The Inn

...to Northumber

Mark Reid

The complete and unique guide
to a circular walk in Northumberland

InnWay Publications

Published by:
INNWAY PUBLICATIONS
102 LEEDS ROAD
HARROGATE
HG2 8HB

ISBN-10: 1-902001-08-7
ISBN-13: 978-1-902001-08-1

www.innway.co.uk

The Inn Way

...to Northumberland

The complete and unique guide to a circular walk in Northumberland

✦

The Inn Way...to Northumberland is a 94-mile (151-km) circular walk divided into six day stages. Detailed maps, route descriptions, fascinating historical quotations, snippets and pieces of information will help guide you through the wild landscape of the Cheviot Hills, the lush Coquet Valley and the sweeping strands of the Northumbrian coastline, passing no less than 48 traditional country pubs and leaving you with a deeper knowledge and understanding of Northumberland.

Weldon Bridge

For Rachel

Thank you to Rachel Gospel, Stewart and Bernadette Reid, Pat and Fi Green, Gareth Latcham, Perry Cleveland-Peck, Matthew Roberts and Geoff Temperton, for accompanying me on many of the walks over the last two years.

I am extremely grateful to the following people and organisations who have helped with my research: Bamburgh Castle, English Heritage, Forestry Commission (Forests of Rothbury), The National Trust, Northumberland County Council, Northumberland Estates, Northumberland National Park Authority, Northumbria Tourist Board and the Otterburn Training Area.

With particular thanks to Tony Derbyshire, Phil Bradley and John McErlane from the Countryside Service at Northumberland County Council, Russell Tait and Kim Hobson from Northumberland National Park Authority, Kevin Redgrave from The National Trust (Northumberland Coast) and Gareth Latcham from the Rose and Thistle at Alwinton.

Front cover photograph: Bamburgh Castle
Back cover photograph: Breamish Valley, Cheviot Hills.
© Julie Fryer, Wigton, Cumbria.

Illustrations © John A. Ives, Dringhouses, York.

Printed and bound by Spectrum Print, Cleethorpes.

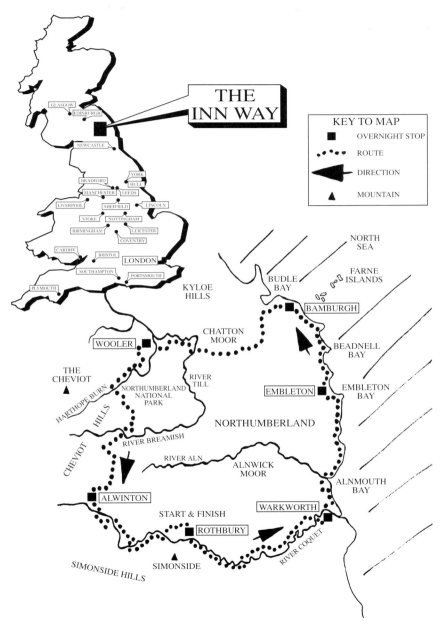

THE
INN WAY

KEY TO MAP

■ OVERNIGHT STOP

•••• ROUTE

◄ DIRECTION

▲ MOUNTAIN

GLASGOW
EDINBURGH
NEWCASTLE
YORK
BRADFORD
HULL
MANCHESTER LEEDS
LIVERPOOL
SHEFFIELD LINCOLN
STOKE NOTTINGHAM
BIRMINGHAM LEICESTER
COVENTRY
CARDIFF
BRISTOL
LONDON
SOUTHAMPTON
PORTSMOUTH
PLYMOUTH

NORTH
SEA

FARNE
ISLANDS

KYLOE
HILLS

BUDLE
BAY

BAMBURGH

CHATTON
MOOR

WOOLER

BEADNELL
BAY

THE
CHEVIOT
▲

RIVER
TILL

NORTHUMBERLAND
NATIONAL
PARK

EMBLETON

EMBLETON
BAY

HARTHOPE BURN

CHEVIOT HILLS

NORTHUMBERLAND

RIVER BREAMISH

RIVER ALN

ALNWICK
MOOR

ALNMOUTH
BAY

ALWINTON

START & FINISH

WARKWORTH

ROTHBURY

RIVER COQUET

SIMONSIDE HILLS

SIMONSIDE

A FOREWORD BY STEVE CRAM

When asked to pen the foreword to this book I did so with the type of mixed feelings that go with finding a fabulous new restaurant whose delights are too good not to share, but hoping that boasting its popularity will take nothing away from its charm. That is Northumberland. A place full of beauty and intrigue, but for me the ultimate attraction is its isolation and serenity.

Too much of my life is spent rushing at brake neck pace to far-flung parts of this shrinking world, however, arriving home is always a joy. Running, walking or biking through this wondrous land is at once, breathtaking (sometimes literally), challenging and an education which Mark Reid brilliantly captures in this marvellous book.

In days gone by, the 94 miles covered would have been an average weeks training. Although the 48 pubs outlined would have been unlikely to figure in most athletes preparations, despite rumours of the odd 'Olympian' drinking sessions. Thankfully these days I'm much more likely to be found walking slowly or supping quietly and if you wish to do the same in one of the best kept secrets of the British Isles then this guide should be your companion.

No place in Britain has more spectacular scenery or indeed more dramatic history displayed within its often altered borders. While much of its beauty is known to me, Mark has managed to embarrass me to delve in more to the characters and events that have left their mark on this part of the world and wider a field. Saints, Viking Marauders, Kings, Dukes, Industrialists and the odd National Heroine have all helped weave an ornate historical tapestry which is expertly depicted. I will now give Earl Grey tea a little more reverence and the next time I 'have a kip' I will be dreaming of stout, Scottish women folk.

So strap on your boots and open your mind. Walk through the beautiful Coquet Valley, get to know the Percys and quench your thirst for life. But if by chance you are standing on the beach in awe of Bamburgh Castle and some lone figure comes running along the sand towards you...it probably won't be me. I'll be in the pub!

CONTENTS

INTRODUCTION

As I sat down to write this Introduction, my mind began to slowly drift through countless days spent walking and researching right back to my first trip to Northumberland. I glanced through my diary to find out exactly when this was and came across four simple words scribbled across the pages of April 2002, words that brought memories flooding back: *"Northumberland, 3 days Rothbury"*. In an instant, I could feel the wind on my face as I picked my way across the heather in search of the famous cup and ring carvings on the weathered sandstone outcrops scattered across the gently rising moorland at Lordenshaws. The memories are all there, waiting for a trigger to bring them vividly back into my mind's eye once again.

Perhaps this is what it has all been about. Over the last two years, I have walked almost 600 miles of footpaths and bridleways and visited almost every pub in north Northumberland. What was once unfamiliar has now become an old friend, with fond memories of seasons and weather, of people and places that have brought so much richness to each and every walk. The experiences, walks and stories have been condensed and pieced together to create this new walk, a walk designed to encapsulate the very essence of Northumberland. It is now time to publish this book and move on. But I am reluctant to leave; the thought has crossed my mind to delay publication until the autumn so I can spend another six months walking the Cheviots, all in the name of research, of course!

It is this reluctance to leave that perhaps speaks loudest about the beauty of Northumberland. For this is a county of wide skies, vast landscapes and far horizons. A landscape of incredibly contrasting scenery with an overwhelming sense of space and solitude that can be found nowhere else; this is England's last true wilderness. But there is more to Northumberland than just the landscape, for people have been living here since the earliest times and their legacy is all around from the mysterious rock art of the 'Black Lands' to the well-preserved Iron Age hill-forts of the Cheviots right through to the medieval castles and pele towers built in response to three centuries of Border bloodshed. The people of Northumberland are genuinely friendly and open, which is reflected in their soft North Country dialect.

I have tried to capture all of these elements in this walk, from the majestic wilderness of the Cheviot Hills and beautiful meandering Coquet Valley to the broad sweeping strands of the coastline. I hope this book will inspire you to discover this Border region for yourself, and return time and again to this 'Secret Kingdom'. I will return to Northumberland; the Cheviot Hills will always be there and, you never know, we may even bump into each other on a walk through Coquetdale one day - if we do, mine's a pint of Best Bitter at the Rose and Thistle.

Hartside

PLAN OF THE BOOK

The Inn Way...to Northumberland will take six days to complete either as a 94-mile circular walk or broken down into individual linear walks of up to twenty miles. Each walk has its own section within this book, designed to provide all of the necessary information for that day's walk. These individual sections contain an information page, route description, hand drawn map and a detailed compilation of information concerning places of interest along the way that are brought to life by a selection of fascinating short quotations from selected travel authors who have visited Northumberland over the last hundred years or more.

Interpretation of Information and Route Descriptions

Walk Information

Points of interest:
This provides a summary of the highlights of the day's walk.

Distance:
The distance travelled in a day has been broken down into 'morning' and 'afternoon' sections with a total mileage for the day. All distances given are 'map miles' estimated from Ordnance Survey (1:25,000) maps. All distances quoted are in miles and yards, conversions as follows:
Yards to metres multiply by 0.9
Miles to kilometres multiply by 1.6
Kilometres to miles multiply by 0.6
Metres to yards multiply by 1.1

Time:
Total time taken to complete the day's walk. This is based upon a walking speed of two and a half miles per hour with consideration for steep ascents, rest stops and viewpoints. This time does not include the obligatory hour lunch break!

Terrain:	Summary of the type of walking surface you will encounter along the way, for example stony tracks, boggy ground etc, as well as any steep ascents / descents and exposed sections.
Ascents:	Each of the major climbs of the day are listed complete with maximum height gained. This figure is not necessarily the total amount of climbing to be done as most ascents start between 50 and 250 metres above sea level. All height figures are in metres (see conversion table above).
Viewpoints:	A selection of the best viewpoints for each section - remember you camera as well as your binoculars for the coastal sections!

Facilities

Inn	See list of 'Public Houses'
B&B	Bed and Breakfast accommodation available in the village.
Shop	At least one shop selling general provisions.
P.O.	Post Office, many of which sell limited provisions.
Café	Teas and light refreshments available.
Bus	Served by public transport, although services are often seasonal and infrequent.
Train	Served by the East Coast Mainline.
Phone	Public payphone.
Toilets	Public conveniences.
Info.	Tourist Information Centres or National Park Information Centres.
Y.H.	Youth Hostel accommodation available in or near the village.
Camp	Campsite in or near the village.

Route Descriptions

The following abbreviations have been used throughout the route descriptions:

SP	Signpost
FP	Footpath
BW	Bridleway
FB	Footbridge
YH	Youth Hostel
Approx	Approximately
UCR	Unclassified County Road

Route finding in Northumberland varies from the well-trodden routes through the National Park and coastal areas to more unfrequented areas such as the lower Coquet Valley and central moorland around Chatton. Thanks to the help and cooperation of Northumberland County Council and the National Park Authority, The Inn Way route should be relatively easy to follow and well marked with signposts and waymarkers. These are often colour-coded as follows: yellow for footpaths, blue for bridleways and red for byways. Some difficulty may be experienced when walking across the Cheviot Hills as there are few landmarks in some of the more remote areas and the path on the ground can sometimes be difficult to discern, however, waymarking throughout the National Park is generally good. This said, always take an OS map and compass with you. The route has been walked several times using solely the route descriptions given, however, to ensure ease of use they should be used in conjunction with the hand drawn maps that appear within the text, with an OS map as back-up. Each route description has been divided into paragraphs that correspond with one of these detailed maps.

RIGHTS OF WAY, ACCESS AND BEACHES

Rights of Way

Public Rights of Way or permitted access areas and footpaths must be used during the completion of this walk. The Inn Way only follows footpaths, bridleways, byways, Unclassified County Roads (UCR) and country lanes, with one or two sections across access land (Forestry Commission) and permissive paths (County Council cycle routes). Footpath repair and conservation work is an important and never ending job and occasionally Rights of Way may be altered or diverted to prevent further erosion damage, to allow areas to regenerate or to simply improve the line of the footpath. Any changes and diversions will be clearly signposted and must be followed.

Beaches

Stage Two and Stage Three of this walk follow the coastal path up from Warkworth to Bamburgh. The route has been described using Rights of Way, which in some sections either run behind large sand dunes or follow the coast road; these are recommended as 'bad weather' alternatives. The best way to complete this walk is by walking along the beaches. Rights of Way or established Access Points onto the foreshore have been described within the route descriptions, thus allowing you to choose your route.

In this country, most of the foreshore (the area between High and Low Water) is the property of the Crown and as such walking, bathing and beachcombing are tolerated although there is no actual legal right to walk along the foreshore; it is also not always safe or passable to do so. There is, however, a public Right of Navigation (by boat) over the foreshore twice a day when it is covered by the tide, and so must be kept open and free from obstruction. In summary, there is generally no problem with walking across the foreshore as long as people use Rights of Way or established Access Points to get on and off the beach. The beaches featured along this walk are well-used and have clear access points therefore you should not experience any difficulties.

The coastline is a constantly changing landscape affected by winds and tides, which may affect footpaths along beaches or cliff-tops - be prepared to alter your route accordingly and follow any diversions. The sand dune ecology is fragile - do not walk across them.

Otterburn Training Area

Stage Six of this walk, from Alwinton to Holystone, follows footpaths and country lanes close to the boundary with (but not into) the 58,000-acre Otterburn MOD Training Area. Much of the area to the south of the River Coquet in Upper Coquetdale (to the south and west of Alwinton) is a live firing area where access is restricted, whilst the area to the north of the river is a 'dry training' area where no live firing takes place and access is open at all times. The Inn Way follows footpaths that are <u>open at all times</u>, however, you may encounter troops and military vehicles - please observe notices and keep to the path.

Spindlestone

THE MAPS

The hand-drawn maps are based upon the Ordnance Survey Explorer (1:25,000) series of maps and are designed to tie in with the route descriptions. The route is easy to follow and is marked by a series of dots along footpaths and bridleways or arrows along roads and tracks (see 'Key to Maps'). Landmarks, places of interest, hills and contours are also given to help you. These maps should guide you safely around The Inn Way…to Northumberland, however, they do not show the surrounding countryside in detail. Should you require detailed information I recommend the following Ordnance Survey maps: -

Ordnance Survey Explorer Map Sheet 325 (1:25,000) 'Morpeth & Blyth'. This map covers the lower Coquet Valley from Rothbury to just beyond Felton (part of Stage One).

Ordnance Survey Explorer Map Sheet 332 (1:25,000) 'Alnwick & Amble'. This map covers Guyzance, Warkworth, Alnmouth, Craster and Embleton. This map also covers Thropton and the area to the north of Rothbury (part of Stage One, all of Stage Two and a small part of Stage Six).

Ordnance Survey Explorer Map Sheet 340 (1:25,000) 'Holy Island & Bamburgh'. This map covers Low Newton-by-the-Sea, Beadnell Bay, Seahouses, Bamburgh, Warenford, Chatton and Wooler (all of Stage Three and Stage Four).

Ordnance Survey Explorer Map Sheet OL16 (1:25,000) 'The Cheviot Hills'. This map covers Wooler, Harthope Valley, Breamish Valley, Alnhammoor, Clennell, Alwinton, Harbottle, Holystone and Hepple (all of Stage Five and most of Stage Six).

Ordnance Survey Explorer Map Sheet OL42 (1:25,000) 'Kielder Water & Forest'. This map covers the area to the south of Rothbury (a small part of Stage Six and Stage One).

KEY TO MAPS

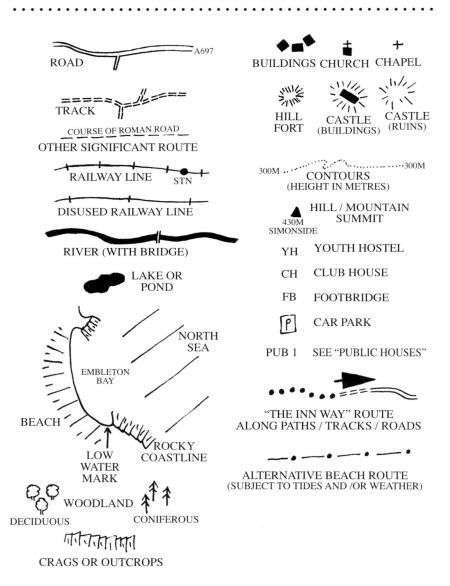

ROAD — A697

TRACK

COURSE OF ROMAN ROAD
OTHER SIGNIFICANT ROUTE

RAILWAY LINE   STN

DISUSED RAILWAY LINE

RIVER (WITH BRIDGE)

LAKE OR POND

NORTH SEA

EMBLETON BAY

BEACH

LOW WATER MARK

ROCKY COASTLINE

WOODLAND

DECIDUOUS   CONIFEROUS

CRAGS OR OUTCROPS

BUILDINGS CHURCH CHAPEL

HILL FORT   CASTLE (BUILDINGS)   CASTLE (RUINS)

300M ⋯⋯300M
CONTOURS (HEIGHT IN METRES)

▲ HILL / MOUNTAIN SUMMIT
430M SIMONSIDE

YH   YOUTH HOSTEL

CH   CLUB HOUSE

FB   FOOTBRIDGE

P   CAR PARK

PUB 1   SEE "PUBLIC HOUSES"

"THE INN WAY" ROUTE
ALONG PATHS / TRACKS / ROADS

ALTERNATIVE BEACH ROUTE
(SUBJECT TO TIDES AND /OR WEATHER)

SAFETY

· ·

• Never underestimate the strenuous nature of walking particularly when this is combined with high ground and the elements. Do not attempt to complete a walk that is beyond your skill, experience or level of fitness.

• Obtain a detailed weather forecast before setting out on your walk. If the weather turns bad then turn back the way you have walked. Conditions can change for the worse within minutes reducing visibility and making walking hazardous with cloud, mist, strong winds and rain virtually all year round. The temperature, wind speed and general weather conditions on exposed moorland, high ground in the Cheviot Hills or along coastal paths can vary significantly from the conditions in sheltered valleys. When walking along beaches, be aware of the tide.

• Take Ordnance Survey maps (1:25,000) of the area. It is essential to carry a GPS (Global Positioning System) or compass as some sections of this walk, particularly through the Cheviot Hills, head through remote countryside with few landmarks.

• Your boots are the most important thing; make sure that they are waterproof, comfortable and have good ankle support and sturdy soles. The wrong footwear can mean every step is blisteringly painful - and you will make over 26,000 strides on a 12-mile walk!

• Waterproof and windproof coat and trousers are essential as well as gloves, hat and fleece for warmth; there is no such thing as bad weather only the wrong clothes!

• Travel light as a heavy rucksack can tire you out, cause backache and make your shoulders sore. Take only essential items such as a change of clothes (remember that several thin layers will keep you warmer than thick bulky layers and take up less room), nourishing snack foods, basic first aid kit, blister plasters, sun cream, whistle, water bottle, torch and 'survival' bag. Line your rucksack with a large plastic bag to keep the contents dry.

• Drink plenty of fluids (not alcohol) and eat food regularly to keep energy levels up.

• Always walk in a group unless you are very experienced and inform someone of your intended route and report your safe arrival. If you are delayed but safe then make sure you let someone know so that a Search & Rescue Team is not called out. In an emergency summon help with six blasts of your whistle or call the Police (who will contact the Search & Rescue Team) giving details of the incident and location.

• Take care when crossing rivers, roads or railway lines and walk in single file (facing oncoming traffic) when walking along country lanes. Do not explore old mine or quarry workings.

• When walking through grassy moorland areas keep a watchful eye for adders, Britain's only poisonous snake. Adders like south-facing slopes and can often be found basking in the sun. Adders will only bite if they are startled or scared - if you are unlucky enough to be bitten seek medical help immediately.

• Above all, keep your hands out of your pockets and look where you are going!

REMEMBER:
"An experienced walker knows when to turn back"

Warkworth

COUNTRY CODE

Tread Gently
Despite surviving all sorts of weather, the hills, their plants and animals are fragile and sensitive. The sand dune ecology is fragile – do not walk across them.

Enjoy the countryside and respect its life and work
Do not touch crops, machinery or livestock and take care not to damage the soil or plants.

Use stiles and gates to cross boundaries
Use stiles and gates to cross fences and walls and close gates behind you.

Keep to public Rights of Way
Footpaths are for walkers; bridleways are for cyclists, horse-riders and walkers. Motorbikes and cars should keep to roads.

Do not make excessive noise
The hill, valleys and coast should be quiet places

Take care on country roads
Face oncoming traffic and walk in single file

Safeguard water supplies
Streams are used by livestock and often feed reservoirs for drinking supplies. Do not foul water supplies.

Guard against risk of fire
Uncontrolled fires can devastate grassy hillsides or moorland, which may never fully recover. Do not start fires or drop matches.

Keep dogs under control
A loose dog can be catastrophic for ground nesting birds, sheep and sometimes the dog itself.

Take litter home
Litter is dangerous and unsightly.

Safety
Weather can change quickly, are you fully equipped for the hills?

USEFUL INFORMATION

If you are travelling by public transport make sure that you check train and bus times before you set out as these often vary seasonally. Book accommodation in advance as B&B's and Youth Hostels can get fully booked up during the summer months and may close temporarily during the winter months.

InnWay Publications Website: www.innway.co.uk
A comprehensive site with detailed information to help organise your walk.

Northumberland National Park Visitor Centres:
Rothbury Visitor Centre   01669 620887
Ingram Visitor Centre   01665 578248
National Park Visitor Centres offer in-depth local knowledge as well as fascinating interpretative displays of the history of the Cheviot Hills and its people through various forms of media. They also form a contact point for the Ranger Service and weather information.

Tourist Information Centres (TIC):
Alnwick   01665 510665
Amble   01665 712313
Berwick-upon-Tweed   01289 330733
Craster   01665 576007
Rothbury   01669 620887
Seahouses   01665 720884
Wooler   01668 282123

Public Transport:
Public Transport Traveline: 0870 608 2 608
A 'one stop' information line for national, regional and local bus and train services. Website: traveline.org.uk

National Express bookings   08705 808080
Rail Enquiries   08457 484950
The nearest railway stations are at Morpeth, Alnmouth or Berwick-upon-Tweed.

Baggage Courier Service:

Brigantes Baggage Courier: 01729 830463
Mr J. M. Schofield
Rookery Cottage
Kirkby Malham
Skipton
North Yorkshire
BD23 4BX
Website: www.pikedaw.freeserve.co.uk/walks

Organisations:

Campaign for Real Ale CAMRA: 01727 867201
230 Hatfield Road
St Albans
Hertfordshire

English Heritage: 0191 261 1585
Northumbria Regional Office
Bessie Surtees House
Sandhill
Newcastle-upon-Tyne
Website: www.english-heritage.org.uk

Forestry Commission *(Rothbury Forest District):* 01434 220242
Forest Enterprise
Kielder Forest District
Eals Burn
Bellingham
Northumberland
Website: www.forestry.gov.uk

Rambler's Association: 020 7339 8500
2nd Floor, Camelford House
87 - 90 Albert Embankment
London, SE17TW
Website: www.ramblers.org.uk

The National Trust   01670 774691
Northumberland Regional Office
Scot's Gap
Morpeth
Northumberland
Website: www.nationaltrust.org.uk

Northumberland County Council   01670 533000
County Hall
Morpeth
Northumberland
Website: www.northumberland.gov.uk

Northumberland National Park Authority   01434 605555
Eastburn
South Park
Hexham
Northumberland
Website: www.nnpa.org.uk

One North East Tourism   08701 601 781
Stella House
Gold Crest Way
Newburn Riverside
Newcastle Upon Tyne
Website: www.visitnorthumbria.com

Otterburn Training Area, Range Liaison Officer 0191 239 4261
Ministry of Defence
Otterburn Training Area
Northumberland

Youth Hostel Association   0870 870 8808
Trevelyan House
Dimple Road
Matlock
Derbyshire
Youth Hostel is located at Wooler
Website: www.yha.org.uk

Weathercall   09068 505 318
Information supplied by Met Office. Premium Rate calls.

**For a detailed accommodation guide send a
Stamped Addressed Envelope to:
InnWay Publications, 102 Leeds Road, Harrogate HG2 8HB.**

Farne Islands

FACILITIES PROVIDED AT EACH OF THE STAGES

Stage One - Rothbury

Rothbury serves as the starting and finishing point because it is easy to get to and has plenty of facilities.

How to get there:

By public transport - the nearest train station is at Morpeth, from where there are frequent bus services to Rothbury. Alnmouth Station lies just off the route of this walk on Stage Two.

By car - from the A697, turn off at Weldon Bridge and follow the B6344 west to reach Rothbury. There is limited long stay parking available at Rothbury, so please make use of the public transport network and save time, money, hassle and the environment!

Facilities - Rothbury is a busy small Northumbrian town set in the beautiful Coquet Valley, serving a wide geographical area. Here you will find a good selection of shops, facilities and amenities including Barclays (cashpoint) and Lloyds / TSB banks, a well-stocked National Park Visitor Centre, outdoor pursuits shop, small supermarket, general stores, Post Office, cafés, bakery, newsagents, traditional ironmongers, chemist, Police Station, telephones, toilets, bus service, car park (limited long stay), campsite and a good selection of hotels, pubs and Bed and Breakfasts.

Stage Two - Warkworth

Warkworth offers Bed and Breakfasts, hotels, bus service, Post Office, general stores and newsagents, telephone, toilets, restaurant, café, bookshop, gallery, antiques shop, gift shops, campsite, Warkworth Castle, Warkworth Hermitage, Fortified Bridge and five pubs.

Stage Three - Embleton

Embleton offers hotel and pub accommodation, Post Office, general stores, café, golf club, bus service, toilets, telephone, campsite (close by) and four pubs.

Stage Four - Bamburgh

Bamburgh offers Bed and Breakfast and hotel accommodation, restaurant, café, greengrocers, garden centre, delicatessen, butchers, gift shops, Post Office, general stores, bus service, toilets, telephone, golf course, campsite (just over a mile from Bamburgh), Grace Darling RNLI Museum, Bamburgh Castle and four pubs. Cashpoint available at Seahouses.

Why not spend an extra night at Bamburgh for a 'rest day', which will allow you time to explore the coast, visit the Castle or take a boat trip out to the Farne Islands.

Stage Five - Wooler

Wooler offers a wide selection of facilities including Bed and Breakfasts, hotels, Youth Hostel, campsites, small supermarkets, Bank of Scotland (cashpoint), Barclays Bank (cashpoint), Post Office, general stores, cafés, fish and chip shop, chemist, bakery, newsagents, greengrocers, delicatessen, antiques and antiquarian bookshop, gift shops, campsite, bus service, Tourist Information Centre & The Cheviot Centre, toilets, telephone, doctors' surgery, Police Station and six pubs.

Stage Six - Alwinton

Alwinton offers Bed and Breakfasts, telephone, Post Office, bus service, car park, toilets, café, campsite (at Clennell) and the Rose & Thistle (evening meals). *Please note: Harbottle is 1.5 miles away from Alwinton (along the route of the next day's walk) and offers Bed & Breakfast (evening meals available), Bunkhouse accommodation and the Star Inn (no accommodation or evening meals).*

All of the above information is for guide purposes only and many facilities are liable to change. **If it is important - check it.**

Felton

PUBLIC HOUSES

The route of The Inn Way…to Northumberland is designed to take in as many of the area's classic country and coastal pubs as possible. There is a wide choice of pubs to suit all tastes ranging from traditional country pubs in the heart of the Cheviots to old fishermen's pubs along the coast, coaching inns along the Great North Road, town pubs and plush hotel bars where you are assured of a warm and genuine Northumbrian welcome. All pubs encountered along the route have been listed - I'll let you make up your own mind as to your favourite ones.

1. Newcastle Hotel, Rothbury: 01669 620334

The Newcastle Hotel stands in the heart of Rothbury overlooking the Lord Armstrong Memorial cross and the old Market Place. It is one of the oldest inns in the town, originally known as the Black Bull, and boasts a comfortable bar as well as a plush lounge / dining room accessible from the central entrance corridor, with its wood panelling and staircase.

ACC / FOOD / TRAD / BAR

2. Turks Head, Rothbury: 01669 620434

This traditional market town pub stands above the sloping tree-shaded green, and is divided in two by a central passageway through which the horse-drawn coaches used to pass to the stabling at the rear; note the datestone of 1874 above the coaching arch. To the side of this passageway is a cosy bar warmed by an open fire.

ACC / FOOD / FIRE / GDN / TRAD / BAR

3. Queens Head, Rothbury: 01669 620470

The Queens Head dates back to the late 18th Century and was originally known as the Golden Fleece, but changed its name to commemorate Queen Victoria's ascension to the throne. In the late 19th Century the hotel was extended, although the original Georgian hotel still forms the right-hand portion of the building. Inside, there is a comfortable lounge bar, with a separate restaurant and games room.

ACC / FOOD / GDN / TRAD

4. Railway Hotel, Rothbury: 01669 620221

This rather unassuming hotel boasts an unspoilt interior with its original layout very much intact, a good example of a traditional town pub with a lounge and separate bar whilst outside there is a large beer garden.

ACC / FOOD / FIRE / GDN / BAR

5. Coquet Vale Hotel, Rothbury: 01669 620305

This large stone-built hotel stands on the south side of the river overlooking the town, a fine example of a Victorian railway hotel built in around 1870 to provide accommodation for travellers arriving on the newly-built railway, when it was known as the Station Hotel. It has recently been refurbished with a ground floor bar and games room, whilst the first floor restaurant boasts original features including ornate cornicing and polished floorboards.

ACC / FOOD / GDN / TRAD / BAR

6. Anglers Arms, Weldon Bridge: 01665 570271

This historic pub dates back to the 1760's when it was built as a coaching inn along the Morpeth to Coldstream road, beside the famous bridge across the River Coquet. This river is renowned for its salmon and trout, indeed the inn has provided hospitality for fishermen (and their tall stories) for generations; the walls are adorned with angling memorabilia as well as several wall-mounted stuffed fish! It is an extremely comfortable inn with a large wood-panelled lounge warmed by an open fire, small bar area as well as a separate dining room housed in an old railway carriage.

ACC / FOOD / FIRE / GDN / TRAD / BAR / INN

7. Northumberland Arms, West Thirston, Felton: 01670 787370

This attractive double bow-fronted old coaching inn overlooks the ancient bridge across the River Coquet linking the hamlet of West Thirston with Felton. The inn once provided hospitality for travellers along the Great North Road, a tradition it maintains. It is a pub of great character and boasts a traditional atmosphere with open fires warming the comfortable lounge and bar, whilst the dining room is housed in the former stables.

ACC / FOOD / FIRE / GDN / TRAD / BAR / INN

8. Stags Head, Felton: 01670 787207

An attractive stone building along the gently rising main road through Felton, this traditional village local has a large lounge bar and a separate games room.

FIRE / BAR

9. Warkworth House Hotel, Warkworth: 01665 711276

This well-proportioned Georgian house was built in 1830 as a private residence for the Forster family. Used during the Second World War as barracks for officers, this fine hotel is famed for its staircase which was brought here from Brandenberg House, Queen Caroline's residence in London, when it was demolished.

ACC / FOOD / TRAD

10. Black Bull, Warkworth: 01665 711367

Featured in the 'Quiet Pub Guide', the Black Bull is a haven of peace and quiet where you can enjoy a pint beside the open fire without the interference of a jukebox, TV or music. The building dates back 300 years and was once used as a candle factory before it became a pub; it is also reputedly haunted by the ghost of a lady. The walls of the bar are adorned with a large collection of fishing flies.

FOOD / FIRE / TRAD

11. Masons Arms, Warkworth: 01665 711398

Overlooking the small market place in the heart of Warkworth, this historic pub was where the Earl of Derwentwater and forty of his followers dined on the 8th October 1715 before proclaiming the Old Pretender as rightful king during the Jacobite Uprising. The L-shaped open plan bar retains some character with oak beams and panelling.

ACC / FOOD / GDN / TRAD

12. Hermitage Inn, Warkworth: 01665 711258

This attractive pub was built in the 1760's originally as a farm / alehouse (animals were once kept in the rooms to the rear) and later doubled as a petrol station for a time! Inside, there are several drinking areas served by a central bar, with traditional yet comfotable décor, stone flags, floorboards, wooden settles and a cast-iron range.

ACC / FOOD / TRAD / BAR / INN

13. *Sun Hotel, Warkworth: 01665 711259*

This imposing and well-proportioned hotel was built in 1825 and has a lovely setting below the magnificent Warkworth Castle. Built using dressed blocks of mellow sandstone, the well-appointed bar of this fourteen bedroom hotel affords great views of the castle.

ACC / FOOD / GDN / TRAD

14. *Hope and Anchor, Alnmouth: 01665 830363*

One of the oldest buildings in the village, the Hope and Anchor boasts a large lounge with comfy sofas, as well as a separate games room and dining room.

ACC / FOOD / TRAD

15. *Sun Inn, Alnmouth: 01665 830983*

The long oak-beamed bar of this traditional village local pub has an open fire at one end and a dartboard at the other, as well as a separate games room; the pubs is buzzing in the evening with darts, pool and quiz nights. Usually opens from 3pm onwards.

FIRE / GDN / TRAD

16. *Saddle Hotel, Alnmouth: 01665 830476*

This unpretentious family-run hotel stands in the heart of the village, with several rooms including a function room, restaurant, lounge and a small but comfortable bar with lots of cosy corners! This traditional yet 'homely' hotel is noted for its home-cooked food, extensive menu and generous portions.

ACC / FOOD / GDN / TRAD

17. *Red Lion Inn, Alnmouth: 01665 830584*

Tucked away through the former coaching arch of this historic 18th Century inn is a cosy wood-panelled bar with old beams, roaring coal fire and old photographs of Alnmouth adorning the walls. The wood panelling reputedly came from the Carpathia, the ship that famously dashed to assist the stricken Titanic.

ACC / FOOD / FIRE / GDN / TRAD / INN

18. Schooner Hotel, Alnmouth: 01665 830216

Known as the 'Famous Schooner Hotel', this old coaching inn is renowned for its ghosts including Parson Smythe as well as other 'spirits' wandering around the bars! There are two lounges and a large conservatory tucked away at the back of the hotel, with interesting bric-a-brac and old photographs of Alnmouth on the walls as well as a range of locally brewed ales.

ACC / FOOD / FIRE / GDN / TRAD

19. Fishing Boat Inn, Boulmer: 01665 577750

This old fisherman's pub enjoys a wonderful location right on the coast in the heart of the old smuggling village of Boulmer, and forms part of the Duke of Northumberland's Estates. In need of modernisation and refurbishment, the Fishing Boat Inn closed during autumn 2003, however, it re-opened in 2005 following major refurbishment. It is now one of the finest coastal pubs in Northumberland with an emphasis on seafood. Wonderful views across the beach from the rear decking area.

FOOD / GDN / TRAD / BAR

20. Jolly Fisherman, Craster: 01665 576461

The Jolly Fisherman dates back to 1847 when Chas Archbald, a local fisherman, decided to open a pub. It retains a great deal of character with a small snug, open fires, lots of fishing and seafaring memorabilia as well as wonderful sea views across the harbour from the back lounge. It is also noted for its crab sandwiches and delicious kipper paté made with the famous oak-smoked kippers from Robson's smokehouse opposite.

FOOD / FIRE / GDN / TRAD / BAR / INN

21. Sportsman Hotel, Embleton: 01665 576588

This imposing whitewashed hotel enjoys a superb location with extensive views from the patio at the front of the hotel, or from one of the window tables inside, across the glorious sand dunes and sweeping beach of Embleton Bay. Inside, the bar is bright and airy with big windows, large tables, an open fire and wooden floors.

ACC / FOOD / FIRE / GDN / TRAD / BAR

22. Dunstanburgh Castle Hotel, Embleton: 01665 576111

This large family-run hotel boasts a restaurant, grill room, cosy lounges warmed by open fires and a small bar tucked away in the heart of the hotel. Across the road there is also a well-kept hotel garden.
ACC / FOOD / FIRE / GDN

23. Greys Inn, Embleton: 01665 576881

Named after the Grey family, this small village 'local' has a cosy atmosphere with an open fire, as well as a games room at the rear; there are distant views of the Cheviot Hills from the beer garden. Note the lovely old "Edinburgh Ales" mirror over the fireplace.
ACC / FOOD / FIRE / GDN / TRAD / BAR

24. Blue Bell Inn, Embleton: 01665 576573

This attractive stone pub was built in the 1850's as a coaching inn, and today offers a warm and friendly atmosphere where locals come in for a chat over a pint beside the coal fire.
ACC / FIRE / BAR

25. Ship Inn, Low Newton by the Sea: 01665 576262

The Ship Inn lies tucked away in the corner of the picturesque square of cottages in this old fishing village. Originally known as the Smack Inn (after the boat!), it dates back to the late 18th Century when the cottages were built for local farm-workers who supplemented their income by fishing in Newton Haven. It is a pub of great character with exposed stonework, floorboards and a pot-bellied stove whilst the large 'green' also doubles as a beer garden. Local seafood features on the menu including lobster from Newton Haven.
FOOD / FIRE / GDN / TRAD / BAR / INN

26. Craster Arms, Beadnell: 01665 720075

Standing proudly in the heart of Beadnell, the Craster Arms is a fine example of a 16th Century pele tower with the coat of arms of the Craster family dominating its stoutly-built frontage. Run by the same family for over fifty years, the lounge bar of this pub is housed in the former stables whilst the beer cellar is in a vaulted room below the defensive tower.
FOOD / FIRE / GDN

27. New Beadnell Towers Hotel (Lobster Pot), Beadnell: 01665 721211

This large imposing hotel dates back to the 18th Century and offers an extremely comfortable lounge, bar, restaurant and no smoking lounge with wood panelling and a large fireplace dominating the main bar; note the interesting bar top with bits and pieces set in resin. The pub has a good reputation for food.

ACC / FOOD / FIRE / GDN / TRAD

28. Olde Ship Hotel, Seahouses: 01665 720200

The Olde Ship Hotel was originally built as a farmhouse in 1745 and obtained its first licence in 1812; amazingly, the pub has been in the same family since 1910. It is an absolute gem with a very distinct 'nautical theme' - it is like being onboard ship! Inside, it is a treasure chest of seafaring memorabilia with its several rooms packed full of nautical knick-knacks... even the wooden floor is made from a ship's deck. Pride of place is the name-board of the 'Forfarshire'. One of the classic pubs of England.

ACC / FOOD / FIRE / GDN / TRAD / BAR / INN

29. Black Swan Inn, Seahouses: 01665 720227

Situated in the historic fishing quarter of Seahouses, this traditional pub overlooks the bustling harbour and is still a favourite haunt of fishermen. After the sinking of the Forfarshire in 1838, the salvage auction was held here.

FIRE / GDN / TRAD / BAR

30. Schooner Inn, Seahouses: 01665 720455

Another old fisherman's pub, the Schooner stands literally next door to the Black Swan behind which were once a dozen herring yards and smokehouses situated amongst a maze of lanes and squares.

ACC / FIRE / BAR

31. Harbour Inn, Seahouses: 01665 720600

This prominent pub stands in the heart of 'new' Seahouses. Built in the 1930's, it is a wonderful example of art deco design that is said to resemble the bridge of a large ship! The curving building houses a lounge, games room and bar.

FOOD / FIRE / GDN / TRAD / BAR

32. *Victoria Hotel, Bamburgh: 01668 214431*

This fine stone-built Victorian hotel overlooks the village green with wonderful views down towards the castle. The bar has a bright airy atmosphere with wooden floors, panelling, comfy chairs, rugs and open fires. To the rear of the hotel is an award-winning brasserie.
ACC / FOOD / FIRE / GDN / TRAD / BAR

33. *Mizen Head Hotel, Bamburgh: 01668 214254*

This large hotel has a distinct 'country house' feel to it, mainly due to the sweeping staircase, parquet flooring and recessed fireplace in the entrance foyer, off which is a snooker room, dining room and a bar with an open fire, exposed stonework and a good range of Real Ales.
ACC / FOOD / FIRE / GDN / TRAD / BAR

34. *The Lord Crewe, Bamburgh: 01668 214243*

This lovely Grade II listed stone-built hotel retains the charm of an old country inn. Named after Lord Crewe who once owned Bamburgh Castle, the hotel is reputedly haunted by his wife Dorothy Forster. There are two lounges to the rear of the hotel with attractive fireplaces as well as an unusual bar-top made up of old pennies.
ACC / FOOD / GDN / TRAD

35. *Castle Hotel, Bamburgh: 01668 214616*

This busy village 'local' dates back to the 1700's when it was built as a coaching inn. Inside, there is a comfortable lounge with a feature stone fireplace as well as a wood-panelled bar area and a rear games room.
FOOD / GDN / TRAD / BAR

36. *Apple Inn, Lucker: 01668 213450*

This cosy country pub was built in the 1840's when it was known as the Apple Tree Inn. Owned by the Duke of Northumberland as part of his Northumberland Estates, the pub boasts wooden floorboards, exposed stonework and a cast-iron stove set in a small inglenook; it also doubles as the village Post Office.
FOOD / FIRE / GDN / BAR

37. *White Swan Inn, Warenford: 01668 213453*

This 200 year old Coaching inn once served travellers along the Great North Road. Inside, there is a large bar with a stone fireplace with steps leading up to the rear lounge and dining room. Excellent reputation for good food.

FOOD / FIRE / GDN / BAR

38. *Percy Arms Hotel, Chatton: 01668 215244.*

This traditional country inn has a lovely setting just up from the green in the centre of Chatton. The L-shaped bar is warmed by an open fire, with a separate snooker room with a full-sized table! Open all day.

ACC / FOOD / FIRE / GDN / TRAD

39. *Tankerville Arms, Wooler: 01668 281581*

Originally known as the Cottage Hotel, this large 18th Century coaching inn is situated just outside Wooler along the Coldstream road. It retains many original features including an impressive array of wall-mounted bells in the hallway, once used to summon room service. The comfortable Copper Bar is warmed by a roaring fire.

ACC / FOOD / FIRE / GDN / TRAD

40. *Red Lion, Wooler: 01668 281629*

This imposing pub appears at first glance to be an old pele tower with its protruding three-storey frontage with two red lion statues. This old coaching inn dates back to 1553, although the frontage is 19th Century, and retains some character with a large stone fireplace in the bar and former stabling to the rear.

ACC / FOOD / FIRE / TRAD / BAR

41. *Black Bull Hotel, Wooler: 01668 281309*

This old coaching inn dates back to the 17th Century, although it was rebuilt in the 19th Century following the famous fire that swept through the town then remodelled again in 1910 when the superb 'Arts & Craft' frontage was added. It retains the atmosphere of an old inn with its coaching arch, large staircase and cast iron fireplace in the front bar.

ACC / FOOD / FIRE / TRAD / BAR

42. *Angel Inn, Wooler: 01668 281573*

The Angel Inn survived the 'great fire of Wooler' and stands as one of the oldest buildings in the town, a rare example of Georgian architecture, although there has probably been a pub on this site since the 17th Century. Inside, it has a bright, modern feel.

FOOD / FIRE / GDN / TRAD / BAR

43. *Wheatsheaf Hotel, Wooler: 01668 281434*

This fine traditional stone-built town pub was severely damaged by fire in 2003. After extensive rebuilding work, the Wheatsheaf re-opened in July 2006 with an updated interior including a large, comfortable open-plan lounge bar and seperate dining room.

ACC / FOOD / TRAD / BAR

44. *Anchor Inn, Wooler: 01668 281412*

This traditional town pub has a small bar and a larger lounge and is popular with locals. It is worth visiting just to see the Gents' ornate porcelain toilets - just make sure you hit the spot!

ACC / FOOD / BAR

45. *Rose and Thistle, Alwinton: 01669 650226*

Tucked away in the heart of Alwinton, this is one of the most remote pubs in Northumberland nestling amongst the beautiful Cheviot Hills in Upper Coquetdale. Its small traditional bar is often busy with farmers and shepherds, whilst the larger lounge affords good views down the valley. The name is said to date from the times when the Border between Scotland and England kept fluctuating so the pub would change its name depending on which country it was in! A classic example of a traditional Northumbrian country pub.

ACC / FOOD / FIRE / GDN / BAR / INN

46. *Star Inn, Harbottle: 01669 650221*

This traditional country pub boasts a cosy bar warmed by an open fire, friendly local chatter and a welcoming atmosphere. There is an emphasis on sports teams, as the many photographs on the walls testify including cricket, pool and darts. The current licensees have been at the pub for over thirty years.

FIRE / BAR / INN

47. Three Wheat Heads, Thropton: 01669 620262

There are superb views from the large beer garden across Coquetdale towards the Simonside Hills. This old stone-built coaching inn dates back 300 years and retains much character with two large stone open fireplaces in the comfortable lounge, as well as an open fire in the restaurant.

ACC / FOOD / FIRE / GDN / TRAD

48. Cross Keys, Thropton: 01669 620362

This village local enjoys an elevated position with views down along the main street through Thropton. There is a small bar warmed by a coal fire and a separate games room.

FOOD / FIRE / GDN / TRAD / BAR

KEY

· ·

ACC	Accommodation
FOOD	Substantial snacks or meals available lunchtime and evening
FIRE	Open real fire
GDN	Beer garden (includes lawns, patios and outside benches)
TRAD	Cask ales available (Real Ale)
BAR	Traditional public bar area
INN	A classic pub.

THE BREWERIES

Good pubs and Real Ale are both in plentiful supply along the coast with a wide range of distinctive, good quality locally-brewed ales on offer. Further inland the situation is quite different, with only a scattering of country pubs around the fringes of the Cheviots where the choice of ale is often limited to keg beers. This Border region is noted for its 'Scotch' style beers; dark, malty brews with a distinctive flavour, a throwback to when the region was one of the last in the country to embrace the use of hops.

Great Britain is renowned throughout the world for its great ales, with literally hundreds of breweries producing thousands of different beers, each with their own distinctive character, flavour, strength and heritage! Well-loved local breweries play an important role in the strong regional identities of this country, with many producing specific styles of beers to suit local palates. With this in mind, I have only listed independent local or regional breweries whose beers reflect the region in which they are sold, rather than national or international brewers who often concentrate on brand image and profit at the expense of regional identity.

Many pubs and inns throughout Northumberland, especially in the more rural areas, are free houses, which means that the licensees are free to choose whichever brand he or she likes. In reality, trade deals and discounts often dictate which products an outlet sells, although the now common 'guest beer' adds variety, all of which means that you may find a whole range of beers on sale that are not listed below.

INDEPENDENT REGIONAL BREWERS

Black Sheep Brewery
Wellgarth, Masham, North Yorkshire

This independent brewery was set up in 1992 by Paul Theakston following the take-over in 1987 of his family firm by Scottish and Newcastle Breweries. The brewery is situated in the former Lightfoot

Brewery maltings literally next door to the offices of T&R Theakston Ltd; Lightfoot's were Masham's 'other' brewery, purchased by Theakston's in 1919. Black Sheep Brewery produces a range of traditional Yorkshire 'style' beers using only the finest ingredients and traditional brewing plant rescued from Hartley's of Ulverston. The pronounced bitterness and characteristic flavour of the beers is reminiscent of some of the old West Riding brews, mainly due to the fact that traditional Yorkshire Square fermenting vessels are used. In spring 2004, a second brewhouse was installed to run in parallel with their existing brewhouse, which will almost double capacity to around 80,000 barrels a year. Black Sheep Brewery only supply to the free trade on a rapidly increasing geographical basis. The Special Ale is a superb example of a Yorkshire strong ale and well worth sampling if you come across it. *Cask ales available include Best Bitter (ABV 3.8%), Special Ale (ABV 4.4%), Emmerdale (ABV 5.0%) and Riggwelter (ABV 5.9%).*

Hadrian and Border Brewery
Hawick Crescent Industrial Estate, Newcastle upon Tyne

Andy Burrows graduated with a degree in Brewing from Heriot-Watt University and, within a few years, bought Border Brewery in 1994. Looking to increase brewing capacity, Andy and his wife Shona bought the plant from Four Rivers Brewery of Newcastle, kept on their beers and formed the new company of Hadrian and Border Brewery in 2000. This small brewery supplies over 100 outlets from the Scottish Borders to North Yorkshire with a legion of followers enjoying their prize-winning beers, many of which have a pronounced hoppy aroma. Look out for Centurion Bitter, Reiver I.P.A. and Secret Kingdom. *Cask ales available include Vallum Bitter (ABV 3.6%), Gladiator (ABV 3.8%), Legion Ale (ABV 4.2%), Centurion Bitter (ABV 4.5%), Farne Island (ABV 4.0%), Flotsam (ABV 4.0%), Reiver I.P.A. (ABV 4.4%), Rampart (ABV 4.8%), Jetsam (ABV 4.8%), Secret Kingdom (ABV4.3%).*

Jennings Brothers
The Castle Brewery, Cockermouth, Cumbria

Cumbria's only remaining independent regional brewer first established in 1828 with brewing taking place at the Castle Brewery since 1874. Jennings became part of the Wolverhampton & Dudley Breweries Group during 2005, however, the future of the Cockermouth Brewery looks assured. A superb selection of real ales is supplied to their estate of 131 pubs and over 300 free trade accounts. Jennings' heartland is the old county of Cumberland, however, recent acquisitions and new free trade accounts have expanded their trading area into Yorkshire, Lancashire, Northumberland and the North East. Cumberland Ale is particularly satisfying after a long day's walk. *Cask ales available include Mild (ABV 3.1%), Bitter (ABV 3.5%), Cumberland Ale (ABV 4%), Cocker Hoop (ABV 4.6%), Sneck Lifter (ABV 5.1%) plus seasonal ales well worth looking out for.*

Mordue Brewery
Tyne Tunnel Trading Estate, South Shields, Tyne & Wear

Garry and Matthew Fawson had been keen 'home brewers' until they discovered that the house they were living in had originally been the Mordue Brewery, which had closed in 1879! They could not let such a coincidence and opportunity pass them by, so decided to start their own brewery using the old Mordue name. Their first beers were Workie Ticket and Five Bridge Bitter, which were launched at the 1995 CAMRA Newcastle Beer Festival where Workie Ticket was voted Beer of the Festival! This exceptional beer then went on to win the prestigious Champion Beer of Britain award at the 1997 Great British Beer Festival, since when the whole Mordue beer range has regularly won awards at beer festivals throughout the country. To cope with demand, they moved to larger premises in 1998 and again in 2005 to a new purpose-built steam-powered brewery at South Shields, which is four times the size of their last brewery. *Cask ales include Five Bridges Bitter (ABV 3.8%), Geordie Pride (ABV 4.2%), Workie Ticket (ABV 4.5%), Radgie Gadgie (ABV 4.8%), IPA (5.1%) as well as a large range of seasonal beers.*

Northumberland Brewery
West Sleekburn Farm, Bomarsund, Bedlington, Northumberland

This microbrewery is sited on the Earth Balance organic farm and was bought by Dave Roberts, a nephew of one of the former owners, in 2002.

They produce an impressive range of beers and supply 100 outlets throughout the North East from Berwick-upon-Tweed to Darlington. *Cask ales available include Castles (ABV 3.8%), Reivers (ABV 3.9%), County (ABV 4%), Kitty Brewster (ABV 4%), Bedlington Terrier (ABV 4.2%), GNC (ABV 4.3%), Best Bitter (ABV 4.5%), Sheep Dog (ABV 4.7%), Bomar Bitter (ABV 5%), Premium (ABV 5%).*

Wylam Brewery

Heddon on the Wall, Northumberland.

John Boyle started this microbrewery in 2000 with Robin Leighton after John had sampled some of Robin's home brew! They set up in an old dairy - the former milking parlour was just perfect for the fermentation and conditioning room. The brewery is slowly expanding to satisfy demand for its range of prize-winning ales, including Turbinia, a rich ruby-coloured hoppy beer, as well as an unusual Bohemia Pilsner. They supply more than 150 local outlets and produce two seasonal beers; Spring Thing (ABV 3.4%) and Wylam Autumn (ABV 4.9%). *Cask ales available include Bitter (ABV 3.8%), Gold Tankard (ABV 4%), Turbinia (ABV 4%), 80/- (ABV 4.5%), Bohemia Pilsner (ABV 4.6%), Haugh (ABV 4.6%).*

THE HISTORY OF NORTHUMBERLAND

It is the rich and diverse landscape of Northumberland that draws visitors to this far-flung county, with dramatic variations from the remote wilderness of the Cheviot Hills to lush pastoral river valleys and the flat coastal plain with its rocky headlands and sweeping beaches. Far from being natural, this landscape has been shaped, moulded and modified since it was first settled by hunter-gatherers some 10,000 years ago - and this process is on-going. Armed with a little knowledge it is possible to interpret this landscape and look through the ages to discover the legacy of the numerous waves of settlers and invaders whose influence on the landscape has fused together over the centuries to form what we see today.

Following the last Ice Age, Stone Age hunter-gatherers roamed through the pristine landscape of thickly wooded valleys and rough hillsides, clearing small areas of land using flints and stone axes. 5,000 years ago, during the late Stone Age (Neolithic) period, these nomadic people began to carve strange shapes across the rocky outcrops of the central sandstone hills. Northumberland boasts some of the finest examples of prehistoric 'rock art' in the world with numerous cup and ring carvings throughout the region; no-one knows their true meaning - they could be astral maps, fertility symbols, religious carvings or waymarkers for people travelling through the area. About 4,000 years ago the stone tools were replaced by more durable metal ones which heralded the onset of the Bronze Age and the dawn of landscape management. These peaceful farmers lived in small communities and began to clear the forests, grow crops and raise livestock. Their legacy can be seen all around with burial mounds, standing stones, clearance cairns and stone circles. During the Iron Age period, which began some 2,500 years ago, the uplands of Northumberland were quite densely populated with numerous large hill-forts, settlements, field systems, dykes and track-ways; these ancient British tribes were collectively known as the Votadini. The Cheviot Hills, and to a lesser extend the central sandstone hills and coastal plain, are littered with countless remains from the Iron

Age with some of the largest and finest hill-forts in the country; their survival is largely due to the fact that this whole area was fought over for many centuries during the Middle Ages whilst in other more peaceful areas of the country farming prospered and many prehistoric remains were swept away by the plough.

Following the invasion of southern Britain in AD43, the victorious Roman Legions pushed northwards from York in around AD80 to capture the lands held by the native British tribes. A military road was built from York to the Firth of Forth, known as Dere Street, which struck a northerly course right through the heart of the Cheviots. Another important Roman military road known as the Stanegate was built along the Tyne Valley to the west thus linking the Roman fort at Carlisle with Dere Street; these roads pre-date Hadrian's Wall. By about AD100 the Roman legions retreated to the Stanegate as they found the troublesome tribes of Caledonia too difficult to conquer, and then in AD122 Emperor Hadrian ordered a wall to be built just to the north of The Stanegate as a visible frontier to separate the Roman Empire from the 'barbarians', although in reality it was more of a frontier control where the passage of people and trade into the Empire could be controlled. Unwittingly, the Romans created the first border in this region, long before England and Scotland ever existed, setting the scene for centuries of conflict between the two countries. The Cheviot Hills and North Pennines boast some of the finest and most spectacular Roman military remains in the world, including the roads of Dere Street and the Devil's Causeway as well as Hadrian's Wall, a World Heritage Site.

Following the demise of the Roman Empire, the British Isles were plunged into what historians call the Dark Ages, however, this term is a misnomer for this was a period of great culture and development that helped shape the Northumbria of today. In the 6th Century, the Saxon chieftain King Ida 'the Flamebearer' landed his ships on the North East coast, quickly conquered the ancient Celtic kingdoms of Northern Britain and built his Royal palace on a great outcrop of Whin Sill at Bamburgh. The Saxon kingdom of Bernicia was born, which later incorporated neighbouring Deira to create an Anglo-Saxon kingdom that stretched from the Firth of Forth to the River Humber that was known as 'North of Humber-land'. His people settled the fertile plains and lower valleys between the Cheviots and the coast in small farming communities paving the way for the settlement pattern we see today; the suffix 'ton' and 'ham' indicate an Anglo-Saxon village. This was a time of great art and culture, noble kings and saints when Christianity flourished in an otherwise pagan Britain - the 'Golden Age of Northumbria'.

This came crashing to and end during the 9th and 10th Centuries with Danish raids from across the North Sea. They took control of Deira and ruled it from York, although Bernicia remained as a Saxon kingdom reduced in size to an area between the rivers Tyne and Tweed. During this period, the emerging kingdom of the Scots, under the leadership of Kenneth McAlpin, took the land between the Forth and Tweed, thus establishing a border that still remains today. Then in the late 11th Century things were to change even more dramatically with the arrival of the Normans. William the Conqueror did not trust the Northumbrians nor the Scots, and his suspicions were confirmed in his eyes when the northern barons rebelled. These rebellions were ruthlessly put down, and the subsequent Harrying of the North laid waste to vast tracts of Northern England, burnt and purged to curb any future insurrection. But the Norman kings needed a strong 'buffer' between Scotland and England so, as this area was too remote to be governed directly, the king carved up the land giving semi-autonomous estates (known as a Liberty) to loyal lords, and established the ecclesiastical 'empire' of the powerful Prince Bishops of Durham. This did little to quell the trouble, made very much worse in 1292 when Edward I chose John Balliol rather than Robert Bruce as successor to the Scottish throne and then demanded recognition as the overlord of Scotland, thus sowing the seeds of three centuries of bloodshed known as the Border Troubles that lasted up until the Union of the English and Scottish Crowns in 1603. During all this instability, the rule of law broke down and families were left on their own to defend themselves. Castles, pele towers and bastle houses were built in virtually every Northumbrian town and village as protection against attack; loyalty was to family names rather than the Crown. Lawless family clans - the infamous Border Reivers - rode out against each other stealing cattle and burning houses in the remote valleys of Redesdale, Tynedale and Coquetdale whilst the Border region itself was terrorised by Scottish raiders. The region was divided into Marches, overseen by Wardens loyal to the King who were meant to bring justice and order but often made things very much worse! The great legacy of this period is the wealth of defensive buildings ranging from the majestic ruins of Dunstanburgh or Warkworth to simple bastle houses such as Woodhouses. Almost all bastle houses are to be found within Northumberland, of which most can be found within twenty miles of the Border.

The Norman lords lived in strong castles and ruled the former Anglo-Saxon kingdom by the sword, whilst the vast majority of ordinary Northumbrians continued to live in the area as they had always done. Their traditions, heritage and culture have survived through the ages, predominantly due to Northumbria's isolation from the rest of the country and its turbulent history, with very few outside influences during the last 1,000 years - who would want to move to Redesdale in the Middle Ages? Perhaps the greatest legacy is the Northumbrian speech, a language rather than a dialect, that is directly descended from Old Saxon with four fifths of words coming from Saxon rather than the quarter in everyday English - have a chat with a local farmer or shepherd to find out for yourself! There is also a great tradition of songs, ballads, dancing and music including the famous Northumbrian pipes.

It took many years, even centuries, for the hills and valleys to recover from the days of the Reivers and Border raiders, however, this lawlessness and fighting helped preserve the wealth of archaeological remains for which Northumberland is now so famous, as the hills and valleys only ever supported a scattering of impoverished farms throughout the Middle Ages.

During more peaceful times in the 18th and 19th Centuries, farmers improved the land and rebuilt their homes, although the solid stark architecture of the bastle houses never went out of fashion. Agriculture slowly prospered, helped by the skill of people such as the Culley brothers of Chatton who helped revolutionise agriculture. Small-scale industry began to emerge including whinstone quarrying, lime production and the development of fishing along the coast, however, the lack of mineral deposits coupled with low population levels meant that the local economy remained dependent upon agriculture, as it still is today. The county has remained largely untouched by industry, with many towns and villages retaining their original layouts including gems such as Warkworth, Alnmouth and Bamburgh. The 20th Century brought with it a growth in tourism with people able to travel quickly and easily by train to the coast and hills. Towns such as Rothbury and Wooler became small health resorts, whilst many tourists flocked to the coast with its wide beaches, bracing air, castles and the famous Farne Islands. The impact of tourism is more noticeable along the coast with its large caravan parks, numerous golf courses and small developments of Edwardian villas and boarding houses on the village fringes. In some areas of the Cheviots the tourists have yet to arrive…

The Northumberland National Park, designated in 1956, covers 405 square miles of diverse countryside ranging from Hadrian's Wall in the south to the Cheviot Hills in the north. It is one of the smallest national parks in England and Wales, the boundaries of which were very skilfully drawn to exclude almost all villages and towns - Harbottle is one of the largest settlements within the Park. It is also one of the least visited National Parks with only 1.5 million visitor days per year, compared to around 22 million visitor days for the Lake District! It must be pointed out that it is neither national nor a park; 56% is under private ownership, 23% is owned by the Ministry of Defence, 19% is owned by Forest Enterprise with the remaining 2% owned by Water Companies, National Trust and the National Park Authority. The National Park Authority is responsible for the management of the park offering advice and assistance to local people and visitors, as well as acting as a planning authority. It has two main purposes:

1. Conserve and enhance the natural beauty, wildlife and cultural heritage of the national Park.

2. Promote opportunities for public enjoyment and understanding of the special qualities of the National Park.

They also have a duty to foster the social and economic wellbeing of local communities.

A very difficult task indeed - it is hard to 'promote' and 'conserve' at the same time! Within its boundaries are some of the finest Roman military remains in the world, a wealth of prehistoric remains, numerous castles, pele towers and bastle houses as well as the remote yet beautiful Cheviot Hills, England's last true wilderness, with the Pennine Way charting a high-level route across the Border Ridge on its final approach to Kirk Yetholm. The MoD Otterburn Training Area covers a huge swathe of land in the centre of the Park, covering some 58,000 acres of desolate moorland and uninhabited valleys; the fact that much of this training area has been closed off from the public for so long, coupled with low intensity farming methods, means that it stands as an area of unspoilt rugged countryside that has become an important habitat for wildlife. Northumberland National Park Authority is leading the way with regards to sustainable tourism and development as they believe that their responsibilities and duties are inter-linked with the well-being of the local economy. The Authority recognises that, as the National Park is a living landscape, there is a mutual dependence between the landscape, environment, local community and rural economy; the only way forward to ensure that this wonderful landscape is preserved and enhanced for future generations is through sustainable development.

But there is more to Northumberland than the National Park. Several rivers rise on the flanks of the Border Ridge flowing west and north to drain into the North Sea, the finest of which is undoubtedly the Coquet which meanders through a deep wooded valley across the heart of Northumberland and the central sandstone hills, or Black Lands, to reach the flat coastal plain and the North Sea. The Northumberland Coast Area of Outstanding Natural Beauty (AONB) was designated in 1958 and covers thirty-nine miles from Berwick-upon-Tweed in the north down to the Coquet Estuary at Amble. This AONB was established to conserve and enhance the natural beauty of the coastline, famed for its sweeping dune-backed beaches, salt marshes, rocky headlands, castles and fishing villages.

We can all help ensure that the landscape, culture and heritage of Northumberland is passed on to the next generation in good working order by embracing sustainable tourism. By spending six days walking through this magnificent Border region, staying overnight in local inns and B&B's, buying food and provisions en route, taking only memories with you and leaving only footprints in your wake, you are making a positive contribution to the upkeep of Northumberland, from the National Park to the coast. A percentage of the profit from the sale of this book will be donated to local conservation projects within the Northumberland National Park; money raised will fund activities such as habitat creation, wildlife surveys or tree planting.

Embleton

THE GEOLOGY OF THE NORTHUMBERLAND

Northumberland is a vast county of incredibly contrasting scenery ranging from broad sweeping beaches to wooded river valleys, rich farmland and wild uninhabited hills. The coastline and the Cheviot Hills are perhaps the best known landscape features of Northumberland, attracting large numbers of visitors who come to marvel at the natural beauty, but what they are looking at is actually the culmination of millions of years of varying influences that have shaped the rocks, which are the foundation of everything we see - without them there would be no vegetation, building materials, coastline, hills or scenery! Armed with a little knowledge about how the landscape has evolved, the countryside through which you will walk along this route will hopefully be viewed in a new light. There are four main areas within north Northumberland: the Cheviot Hills, the surrounding lowland fringes, the central sandstone moorland and the coastal plain. To understand how these hills, valleys and coastline were formed we need to look back to the dawn of time when the first rocks were created.

During the Devonian period some 400 million years ago, the area now occupied by Northumberland was covered by a vast sea sandwiched between huge mountain ranges. Then, around 380 million years ago, violent eruptions from deep within the earth sent molten rock, ash and lava spewing across the area - the Cheviot Hills had begun to take shape. A great mountain range of igneous rock was created topped by thick drifts of lava, known as andesite, which had pushed up under great force through the earth's crust and spread out across the volcanoes. After a lull of around 10 million years, a great 'plug' of molten rock intruded into the very heart of this savage landscape, then cooled to create a central core of granite (the present-day Cheviot massif). As this huge mass of molten granite intruded into the lavas, the intense heat literally baked the adjacent lavas to create a harder ring of 'baked' andesite rock. Almost 400 million years later, this slightly more resistant rock now forms a huge ring of 'tors' around the central granite core. But the great domed hills of the Cheviots we see today are not extinct volcanoes. The thick andesite 'cap' has eroded down over millions of years leaving the granite core of the Cheviot massif surrounded by a thick nutrient-rich layer of soil created from the weathered andesite covering a range of rounded closely-grouped hills. Today, the prominent feature of these hills is grassland of bleached mat-grass and fescue, which gives the whole area its distinctive character - the 'White Lands'.

Around the foothills and fringes of the Cheviots runs a wide sweeping swathe of undulating rich farmland including the Vale of Whittingham and Milfield Plain. These are the Cementstone Group of rocks laid down some 300 million years ago during the early Carboniferous period, which form a distinctive divide between the central sandstone Black Lands and the White Lands of the Cheviot Hills. These rocks consist of layer upon layer of sandstone, clay, shale and limestone deposited by torrents of water flowing down from the newly created volcanic landmass of what are now the Cheviot Hills into a surrounding deep sea. The Cementstone rocks are easily weathered and so have produced the fertile undulating lands around the eastern edge of the well-defined Cheviot range.

Millions of years later, a thick band of sandstone was deposited above these Cementstone rocks in a huge river delta, which was subsequently pushed and tilted by a series of massive earth movements that created the central sandstone hills with their west-facing escarpments. These hills form a natural upland barrier between the flat coastal plain and the lush vales on the eastern fringes of the Cheviot Hills. From the Kyloe Hills to the north of Belford, these heather-clad moors swing southwards forming a series of ridges and broad swathes of heather moorland including Chatton Moor, Bewick Moor and Alnwick Moor before curving west to form the Simonside Hills and Harbottle Hills. These hills are known as the 'Black Lands' due to their acidic peaty soils and heather moorland vegetation covering the underlying Fell Sandstone rocks and have their own distinctive character with broad moorland ridges that shelve gently towards the coastal plain whilst their western slopes rise sharply with steep escarpments and rocky outcrops facing the Cheviots.

One of the jewels in the geological crown of Northumberland is the magnificent coastline. Here you will find mile upon mile of sweeping strands, broad estuaries, high sand dunes, rocky headlands and islands. The underlying rocks were laid down during the late Carboniferous period and are comprised predominantly of layers of limestone along with thin seams of coal, shale, sandstone and the narrow dyke of whinstone, perhaps the most striking feature of the coast. This dramatic intrusion of dolerite rocks was formed by volcanic activity some 280 million years ago when this extremely hard igneous rock pushed up between the existing Carboniferous limestone strata. The Great Whin Sill can be traced right across the county from Lindisfarne down along the coast to just south of Craster before striking south west appearing as a long ridge of crags above the Tyne Valley. As it is harder than the surrounding rocks, it has weathered more slowly producing a hard ridge of rock prefect for castles such as Bamburgh and Dunstanburgh.

Over millions of years the forces of nature - wind, rain, frost and sun - have eroded and shaped this landscape. Perhaps the most important of these was the Ice Age, which lasted for a period of around 2 million years with the ice advancing and retreating on several occasions, the last retreat being about 10,000 years ago. The ice smoothed the river valleys, dropped thick deposits of boulder clay and glacial drift, scoured out meltwater channels and formed vast lakes. This process of erosion continues; the landscape is constantly evolving and changing.

FAUNA AND FLORA

Due to the varied geology, geography and climate of Northumberland there is an enormous diversity and abundance of plants, flowers, birds, insects and animals, most of which can be enjoyed at first hand by the observant walker.

The granite Cheviot massif, the highest ground in Northumberland, is topped with a thick blanket bog that supports purple moor-grass and heather, whilst the surrounding andesite White Lands are covered with hardy coarse grasses such as fescue, bent and mat grass. With few walls or fences, the vast grass-covered open landscape is superb sheep country with local breeds such as the Blackface and Cheviot roaming across the hills. This stunning 'prairie' landscape makes for ideal walking country but is not particularly rich in wildlife, although the rough grassland provides the perfect spring nesting sites for upland birds such as golden plover, lapwing and curlew (the emblem of the National Park) as well as several other smaller birds such as the meadow pipit, skylark and wheatear, whilst predators circle above such as hen harrier, peregrine falcon, merlin and kestrel. In the unfrequented valleys high on the Border Ridge are small herds of elusive wild goats. Great swathes of hill-country has been cloaked in coniferous plantations, which provides cover for deer, fox and red squirrel as well as woodpecker, sparrowhawk, tawny owl, redstart, goldcrest, siskin and crossbill. In the more remote areas of the Cheviots in steep-sided ravines and beside tumbling burns are pockets of primeval woodland that once would have covered the slopes and valleys following the last Ice Age with alder, birch, hazel, oak and juniper.

The upper slopes of the central sandstone hills are covered by heather moorland, its dark forbidding appearance comes to life for just a few short weeks each year during late summer when millions of purple flowers come into bloom, attracting thousands of bees. The hardy bilberry bushes can often be found amongst the heather, the succulent fruit a local delicacy in home-made pies. On south-facing slopes you may also catch a glimpse of an adder, slow-worm or a common lizard, whilst across the moors you will find rabbit, hare, weasel, stoat, foxes, mice, voles and shrews.

Several large rivers rise on the hills, flowing north and eastwards through thickly wooded valleys where kingfisher and heron fish, trout and salmon swim and otters hunt; the National Park has the cleanest rivers in England. Ancient woodland cloaks the riverbanks and supports a profusion of wild flowers such as great willow-herb, purple loosestrife, meadowsweet, water aven, bluebell, red campion, dog's mercury, primrose, wood anemone, lady's smock, birdsfoot trefoil, common dog violet, wood sorrel, ragged robin, wild garlic and foxglove a common sight. Birds such as dipper, grey wagtail, pied wagtail, grey heron, spotted flycatcher, stonechat, sandpiper, housemartin, swallow, mistle thrush, wren, great tit, coal tit, willow warbler, treecreeper, bullfinch, blackcap, woodwarbler, goldfinch, great spotted and green woodpecker can be seen along the wooded riverbanks and around the broad estuaries. Amongst the undergrowth you may see bagder, red squirrel, fox and roe deer.

The coastline is perhaps the finest area for wildlife with several important Nature Reserves such as the Farne Islands, Budle Bay and Beadnell Bay offering a diverse range of habitats from sea-cliffs to mud flats, salt march, tidal estuaries and sand dunes. These habitats in turn support a profusion of birds including waders such as oystercatcher, redshank, dunlin, curlew, turnstone, ringed plover, greenshank whilst the sea-cliffs and rocky headlands support vast colonies of guillemot, fulmar, tern, shag, cormorant, eider duck, kittiwake and puffin with grey seal often basking on the shelving rocks. The fragile sand dunes support important plants such as bloody cranesbill, burnet rose and several species of orchid.

Rothbury

STAGE ONE

ROTHBURY
to
WARKWORTH

✦

"A sylvan riverside path leads down from the famous Warkworth Hermitage alongside the broad Coquet then, all of a sudden, a stone fortress comes into view towering above the trees, a bold statement of Northumbrian strength and power designed to intimidate potential invaders and plunderers from across the Border. Here, more than anywhere else, you sense history all around… you get lost in your thoughts and soon start to imagine medieval soldiers on sentry duty high on the castle ramparts, keeping a watchful eye for Scots. The town is a gem, still on its original medieval layout, with the Castle dominating and a fortified bridge protecting the town's northern approaches. Just down from the Castle is a wonderful old church with a very sad tale to tell and an old inn, where Jacobite plotters met. Few places have the power to transport you back in time - enjoy the journey."

Mark Reid
March 2003

WALK INFORMATION

Points of interest:

Anglo-Saxon Rothbury Cross, Armstrong the 'gun-maker', walking the Coquet Valley, Brinkburn Priory and the resting place of the Northumbrian fairies, heugh and haugh farms, old coaching inns, ancient woodland, the Great North Road, England's finest weir, monastic remains of Guyzance, a hermit's house and magnificent Warkworth Castle.

Distance:

Rothbury to Weldon Bridge	6.5 miles
Weldon Bridge to Felton	4.5 miles
Felton to Warkworth	6.5 miles
Total	17.5 miles

Time:

Allow 7 - 8 hours

Terrain:

This walk follows the banks of the River Coquet virtually all the way to Warkworth passing through woodland and across pastureland, parts of which may be wet and muddy after heavy rain. There are some short sections along quiet country lanes around Guyzance. The A697, A1 and East Coast Mainline are crossed via two underpasses and a bridge.

Ascents:

No significant ascents along this walk - gently does it on the first day!

Viewpoints:

Looking across the Coquet Valley from Craghead.
Glimpses of Brinkburn Priory through the trees from the wooded riverside banks above Middleheugh.
Warkworth Castle from the riverside path.

FACILITIES

Rothbury	Inn / B&B / Shop / P.O. / Café / Bus / Phone / Toilets / Info. / Camp
Pauperhaugh	Phone / Bus
Weldon Bridge	Inn / Bus
Felton	Inn / B&B / Shop / P.O. / Café / Bus / Phone
Warkworth	Inn / B&B / Shop / P.O. / Café / Bus / Phone / Toilets / Camp

ROUTE DESCRIPTION

(Map One)

Starting from the Armstrong Memorial Cross in the centre of Rothbury, head out of the corner of the Market Place along Church Street (passing the Parish Church on your left) bearing round to the left along Haw Hill to reach a T-junction, where you turn right over the bridge across the River Coquet. After the bridge, follow the main road to the left gradually climbing up then, just after the Fire Station, turn left along Wagtail Road. Follow this road down out of Rothbury to reach a junction of lanes beside some old bridge supports (bridge missing). Head straight on through the gate (SP 'West Raw') along a clear track then, where this bends sharply down to the left, follow the track to the right ahead (waymarker) that leads on (Wagtail Farm across to your right) down to reach Little Mill beside the River Coquet. Pass to the left of the house just after which bear right to a stile over a fence, after which head straight down to reach the river. Head straight on along the riverside path then, as you reach the first small island in the middle of the river, head to the right (waymarker) up through the woods (leaving the riverside behind). Follow the path gradually bearing up through the woods (waymarkers) then, after a while, the path heads straight on dropping down very slightly across an area of boggy ground before slanting up once again through the trees to emerge from the woods. Head up across the steep grassy bank to join the stone wall on your right which you follow on to reach a stile over a fence (at the top of the bank). Head straight on alongside the fence / old railway line on your right for a short distance then, at the gate on your right, continue on bearing slightly to the left across the field to reach the ruined Craghead Farm. Pass to the right of the old farm and follow the rough track on through a series of gates to reach West Raw Farm. As you reach the farmyard, follow the clear track to the right skirting around the barns then right again at the farmhouse on to join a road on a bend. Turn left here through a gate (SP 'Pauperhaugh'), then head straight on along a rough track to reach an old cottage. Turn left through the first gate immediately after the cottage (passing in front of the cottage), then head on with the fence on your right following the field boundary bending round to the right, through a gate and continue on, then at the end of the field (at the top of the wooded bank) head to the left to a bridle-gate that leads into woodland. Follow the clear path down to a gate at the end of the woods, then head straight on across the field to reach the banks of the River Coquet. Turn right alongside the river / fence to reach the road beside Pauperhaugh Bridge.

(Map Two)

Turn right along the road and follow it gently curving round to the right then take the path to the left over a FB across Forest Burn (SP 'Thornyhaugh, Weldon Bridge'), after which turn left along a grassy track, over a stile beside a gate then continue straight on alongside the fence on your right passing to the left of Longhaugh Farm (ruin), immediately after which head straight on to reach the banks of the River Coquet. Turn right along the riverside path then, at the end of the field, head right to quickly reach a gate. Follow the rough track climbing up to reach a junction of tracks beside Thornyhaugh Farm. Turn left along the track passing the barns on your left then head through a gate behind the farmhouse that leads through the yard to quickly reach another gate out onto a field. Head to the right across the field, keeping fairly close to the fence on your right, down to a FB across Maglin Burn. After the FB, head straight up the hillside to the top of the bank then straight on across the field to a stile / gate in a fence just after a small stream, after which continue on bearing slightly to the left through a bridle-gate in the far left corner of the field (above Middleheugh Farm) and down onto a track. At the track, cross the stile just beyond the small pond (do not enter the farmyard), then head up across the field to a bridlegate in the top left corner (where the hedge meets the woodland). Head straight on with the fence / woodland on your left, through another bridlegate then over a stile, after which turn left (still with the woodland on your left) along the edge of the field gradually dropping down then, at the end of the field, head through the gate just to your right down to reach Brinkheugh Farm. Head through the gate onto a track behind the farmhouse and follow this track bending to the left out of the farmyard. Continue along this track passing to the right of the brick-built barn then down to join the bottom of a metalled lane. Follow this road straight on (passing the turn for Thistleyhaugh Farm) then where this road forks follow the left-hand branch down to a bridge across Tod Burn. Take the FP to the left immediately before this bridge (SP 'Weldon Bridge') and follow the path on alongside the fence on your left climbing up a gorse-covered bank to reach a stile beside the metal gate to your left, after which turn right alongside the fence / hedge on to reach a farm lane. At the lane, head through the gate opposite, then head to the right across the field to join the fence on your right that quickly leads on to a gate in the far right corner of the field. Continue straight on alongside the fence down to a FB across Tod Burn, after which follow the clear path through woodland alongside the River Coquet to reach the road beside Weldon Bridge.

(Map Three)

Turn left over Weldon Bridge then follow the road straight on, passing the Anglers Arms on your left, up to reach a T-junction with the B6344. Turn right along the road passing through the underpass beneath the A697 and follow the road bending round to the right then turn left on this bend along a clear track through a gate (before you reach the

A697). Follow this track straight on then bending up to the left to reach Low Weldon Farm. Follow the track passing to the left of the house then bending round to the right, through a small gap after which follow the clear enclosed path (woodland on your right) straight on then bending to the left up to reach High Weldon. Walk straight on passing between the buildings (house on your right) then straight on down through a small gate onto a stony track. Follow this clear track straight on passing a large barn then bending round to the right down to reach a gate. After the gate, the track leads on across open pastures bending to the left to reach a large house. As you approach the house, head through the bridle-gate beside the cattle grid (ignore the bridge to the right), after which turn left climbing up the hillside along a grassy path then, at the top of the bank, follow the path bending round to the right (waymarkers) on through a bridle-gate then continue on along the top of the wooded banks above the River Coquet to another bridle-gate at the end of the woods. Turn right along the field-edge with the fence / woods on your right to another bridle-gate then head straight on across the field along the top of a low 'ridge' to a stile beside a gate by a fence corner. After the stile, head straight on alongside the fence on your right to a stile at the end of the field, then continue on to reach a gate that leads onto the driveway just to the left of Elyhaugh. Cross the driveway and head through the gate immediately to the right of the cattle grid then bear to the right around the buildings, down a bank to join a track that leads down to a gate and a riverside track. Follow this track on then, at the ford, head up to the left to quickly reach a stile (SP 'Felton'). Cross the stile then turn right alongside the fence / river on your right. Follow this riverside path gently curving round to the left then climbing up a grassy bank, still keeping close to the fence on your right, passing a bench to reach a gate (waymarker). After the gate, bear right down across the rough hillside (waymarkers) to join the fence / riverbank on your right and follow this on over a small side-stream, after which head up a small bank then where this levels out (marker-post) head on to the right, keeping close to the wooded riverbank on your right at first, then bear slightly to the left on to reach a junction of 'paths' (marker-post) where you head straight down to reach a FB across Swarland Burn.

After the FB, follow the path to the right then as you reach the river turn left and follow the clear path up to quickly reach a wide track. Turn right along this track and follow this clear track (ignore the path off to the left) climbing up through the woods then levelling out - continue straight on along this track across the top of Mill Banks (river down to your right) until you reach a bridle-gate across your path beside the A1 road bridge (ignore gate to your left). Head through this bridle-gate down beneath an underpass below the A1 then up some steps on the other side through another bridle-gate to the right of a bench, then follow the clear path straight on through woodland along the top of the steep bank (River Coquet down to your right) to reach a kissing gate at the end of the woods. Follow the grassy track straight on across the field to join a clearer track that leads on through a gate to join a road opposite St Michael's Church. Turn right down along the road then at the T-junction turn right into the centre of Felton.

(Map Four)

At the T-junction in the centre of Felton (Felton Bridge just to your right) turn left up along the Main Street (SP 'Alnwick') passing the Stags Head on your left then turn right along Mouldshaugh (a wide gap between the houses opposite Park View - SP 'Mouldshaugh Lane, River Coquet'). Follow this lane straight on out of Felton and on to reach the farm buildings at Mouldshaugh. As you reach the farm buildings follow the track to the left of the large corrugated barn then, almost immediately, bear to the left diagonally across the field along a clear narrow path (passing to the left of the solitary tree) to reach the wooded banks of the River Coquet in the far corner of the field. Follow the path down over a small FB across a side stream then through a kissing gate, after which continue straight on alongside the fence / river on your right to reach a stile that leads into woodland. Follow the clear path straight on along the wooded banks of the river, over two small footbridges after which the path gradually climbs up through the woods to join the fence at the top of the wooded bank which leads on to reach a small FB / stile at the end of the woods. After the stile, head right alongside the fence on your right along the top of the wooded ridge, through a bridle-gate then on to reach a stile (woodland ends on your right). After this stile, turn left alongside the fence on your left, through a series of gates then follow the fence as it bends round to the left on to reach a stile beside a gate which leads onto a track (SP). Turn right along the track passing Waterside Cottage (River Coquet on your right) to join a road. Turn right along the road, over a road-bridge and follow the road round to the right towards 'Guyzance, Acklington' then, after a short distance, take the FP to the left over a stile (SP). Head diagonally to the right across the field (passing the solitary tree) on to reach a stile in the far right corner that leads down through woodland onto the road. Turn left and follow the road alongside the River Coquet at first then climbing up to reach a road junction where you follow the road up to the right into Guyzance. Follow the road through Guyzance then bending round to the left out of the village and continue on for about half a mile then turn right along a track just before East House Farm (SP 'Brotherwick'). Walk along the track, through a gate then straight on across the small campsite (house across to your left) to a stile in the bottom corner of the field. Continue straight on alongside the hedge on your right, crossing the line of an overgrown hedge at the end of the field then continue straight on passing an electricity pylon then, as you approach the end of this field, turn left (waymarker post) across the field to reach a stile that leads into woodland. Walk through the woodland to quickly emerge out onto another field, where you turn left alongside the hedge to reach a gate that leads onto the road at a junction.

(Map Five)

At this junction, turn right (SP 'Coquet Moorhouse') and follow this road straight on over a bridge across the East Coast Main Line then continue on for about half a mile then take the FP to the left (SP 'Heather Leazes') just before the caravan park. Follow the enclosed path down then through a gate to the right that leads out onto the caravan park, then bear to the left through the caravan park to reach a gate at the other side that leads onto a riverside path. Turn right and cross the FB across the River Coquet, after which follow the road to the left climbing up then levelling out into Heather Leazes. Continue along this road then where it bends sharp right, take the turning to the left. Follow this lane down then where it divides (beside the stone cottage of Howlet Hall) bear right (SP 'Hermitage, Warkworth') down to reach the River Coquet. As you reach the river and the mooring for Warkworth Hermitage, turn right along the riverside path (SP) and follow this clear path alongside the gently curving river (Warkworth Castle soon comes into view). As you reach the foot of the steep slope beneath the castle, follow the clear path slanting up (SP 'Warkworth Castle') passing beneath the ramparts to reach the top of Castle Street in the centre of Warkworth.

Rothbury

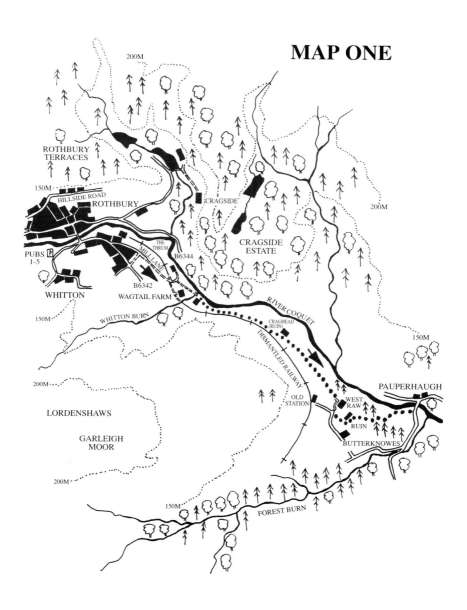

MAP ONE

200M

ROTHBURY
TERRACES

150M

HILLSIDE ROAD

ROTHBURY

CRAGSIDE

200M

PUBS
1-5

THE
THRUM

MILL LANE

B6344

CRAGSIDE
ESTATE

B6342

WHITTON

WAGTAIL FARM

150M

WHITTON BURN

RIVER COQUET

CRAGHEAD
(RUIN)

150M

200M

DISMANTLED RAILWAY

LORDENSHAWS

OLD
STATION

WEST
RAW

PAUPERHAUGH

RUIN

GARLEIGH
MOOR

BUTTERKNOWES

200M

150M

FOREST BURN

MAP TWO

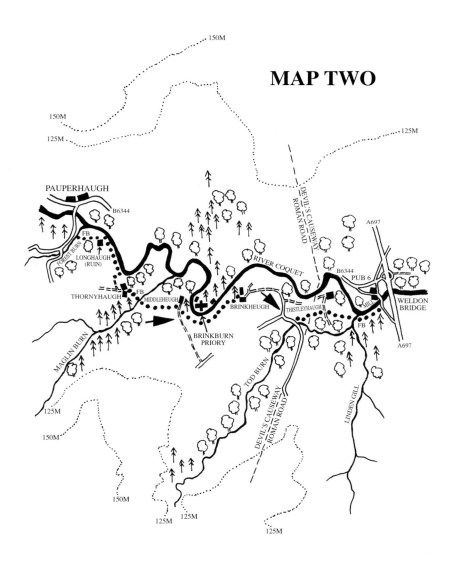

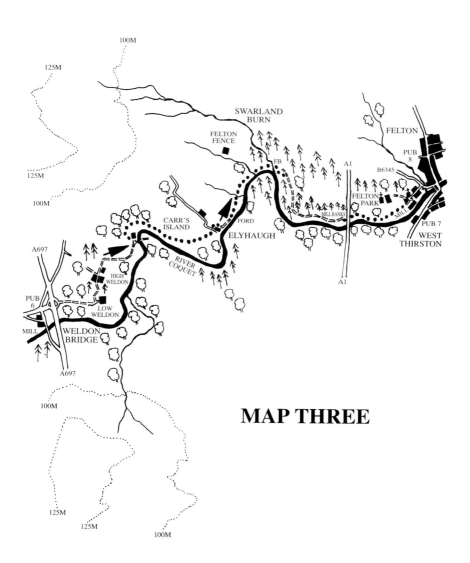

MAP THREE

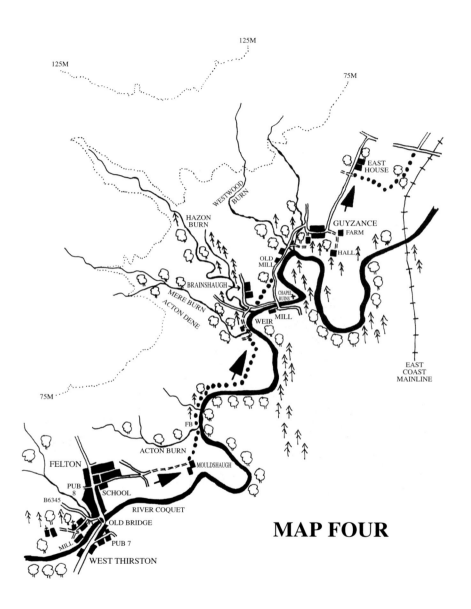

MAP FOUR

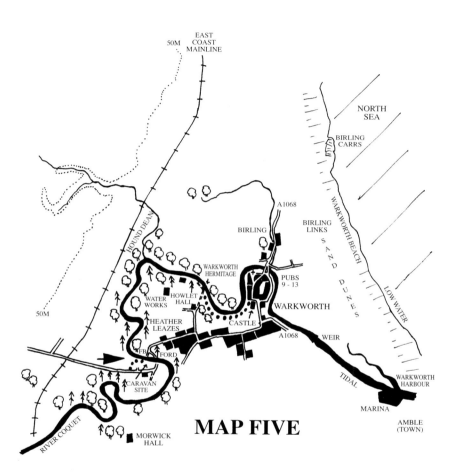

MAP FIVE

ROTHBURY is a traditional old Northumbrian market town of mellow stone buildings set around a long and sloping tree-shaded green, often referred to as the 'capital of Coquetdale' and gateway to the Northumberland National Park. It is surrounded by some of the finest countryside in England with the mysterious Simonside Hills to the south, magnificent Cragside Estate and the Rothbury Terraces to the north and Upper Coquetdale snaking its way westwards towards the remote yet beautiful Cheviot Hills. Situated in a narrow part of the valley with its feet dipping in the River Coquet, Rothbury is hemmed in by heather-clad hills, indeed, most of the streets run east to west, taking advantage of natural 'terraces' of land. *"Descending upon Rothbury from the high ridge of the lonely moorland road to Alnwick, more especially in stormy weather, the whole situation suggests the conventional, though somewhat banal epithet of "alpine", more than any spot frequented by man in all Northumberland. This is due, in part, to the fine rugged summits of Simonside and Tosson hill. But the deep gorge in which Rothbury nestles presents altogether a fine effect, opening westward to meet the Coquet as it comes gleaming down through green meadows, yet so greatly narrowing below the town that for some distance the high road is cut into the steep wooded hills of Cragside, Lord Armstrong's seat, while the river boils in rocky pools below".*
(A. G. Bradley 'The Romance of Northumberland' 1908.) People have been living in this area since prehistoric times, indeed this area boasts a wealth of Stone, Bronze and Iron Age remains including the famous hill-fort and cup and ring marked stones at Lordenshaws on the flanks of the Simonside Hills. This long ridge of sandstone hills, punctuated by rocky outcrops, was an important site for the ancient British tribes who lived in this area thousands of years ago. It is little wonder that superstitions have grown up around these hills including the belief that they are the haunt of spirits, giving rise to the legend that Simonside is a sacred mountain. There has been a settlement and church at Rothbury since Anglo-Saxon times, however, it was following the Norman Conquest that the town began to develop as a trading centre protected by a castle. In 1205 King John granted his Manor and Forest of Rothbury to Robert Fitz-Roger, the Baron of Warkworth, which passed to the Percy family (Earls of Northumberland) in 1332; the

present Duke of Northumberland is still the Lord of the Manor and owns large tracts of land in the area. In medieval times, the town was little more than a collection of heather thatched cottages lining the long green, at the east end of which was the stone-built church and castle; many cottages were still thatched well into the 19th Century. The castle originally stood on Haw Hill overlooking the river and was still standing, albeit in a ruinous state, in 1869 when it was demolished to make way for a new churchyard; no trace of the castle remains. In 1291 Edward I granted the town a Market Charter, allowing a weekly market and annual fairs. This old Market Cross was demolished in 1827 and later replaced by the present finely carved Lord Armstrong Memorial cross in 1902. It was near to this old Market Cross that the pillory, town stocks and bull-baiting ring were located; the last person to be put in the stocks was in 1820 for being drunk and disorderly. In olden times, Rothbury had a rather bad reputation for rowdy behaviour, poaching, cock-fighting and general lawlessness, indeed, in the 18th Century there were five cock-pits in the town! *The people of Rothbury in former times were amongst the wildest and most uncivilised in the county. For fighting, gaming, and drinking they had a worse reputation than the inhabitants of Tynedale and Redesdale.* **(William W. Tomlinson 'Comprehensive Guide to Northumberland', 1888).** All Saints Church stands on the site of an 8th Century Anglo-Saxon monastic church, which was much bigger than the present church stretching to the west across Church Street. This early church was destroyed by Vikings and lay in ruins until the 13th Century when a new church was built on the eastern part of the original foundations. Extensive restoration work in 1850 swept away much of the medieval masonry, with the exception of the chancel arch. Inside the church you will find the richly carved Rothbury Cross, one of the finest Saxon crosses in existence dating from about 800AD and featuring the earliest carving of the Ascension in this country. The shaft of this Cross now forms the pedestal of the font, which dates from 1664. In the churchyard on Haw Hill are the graves of the Armstrong family including the 1st Lord Armstrong as well as the beautifully carved headstone of Walter Mavin, 'The Coquet Angler', who was the fishing companion of Lord Armstrong. The town's heyday was during the 19th

Century following the arrival of the railway that brought tourists to the area for the fresh country air, fishing along the Coquet, attractive countryside, racecourse and Cragside; the town became something of a health resort. The Rothbury Branch Line was built in 1870 by the North British Railway Company and ran from Rothbury to Scot's Gap where it joined the Morpeth to Bellingham line. *"Its charming and romantic situation, sheltered from the cold east winds by rugged and picturesque hills, with its clear, bracing air, its wild mountain scenery, with fishing in the most beautiful of Northumbria's streams – the Coquet – and its close proximity to the lovely grounds of Cragside, at once offers attractions which no other locality in the north of England can surpass. There is ample accommodation in the town for all classes."* **(David Dippie Dixon 'Upper Coquetdale' 1903.)** The large flat area of land to the south of the river, now occupied by the Golf Club, was the site of Rothbury's Racecourse from 1762 until the last race meeting was held in 1965. The closure of the railway and racecourse in the 1960's meant that several large hotels closed their doors including the County Hotel, which became a miners' retirement home and then a RAFA home. Other buildings of note include the Parish Hall, just to the north of All Saints Church, which was built in 1908 on the site of the Three Half Moons pub. This was once the principal pub in the town where meetings and courts were held and where the Earl of Derwentwater stayed before going to Warkworth where he proclaimed the Old Pretender as the rightful king during the Jacobite Rising of 1715; only the 17th Century doorway of the pub was left standing. The ancient bridge across the River Coquet was originally built as a packhorse bridge in medieval times, although it was extended in the 16th Century and then widened in 1759 when the Corn Road between Hexham and Alnmouth was constructed. The Corn Laws were introduced during the 18th Century in response to a growth in the population as well as exports to new-found colonies. They were designed to promote production of corn by imposing duties on imports, thus maintaining prices, although the laws were criticised as protecting the landed gentry at the expense of the poor. The bridge is a Scheduled Monument, despite its modern road-deck. Just to the east of Rothbury lies Cragside, a vast estate of mature woodland, lakes and driveways at the heart of which is a magnificent Victorian country house. The Cragside Estate was bought and developed by William Armstrong (1810 - 1900) during the 1860's as a modest country retreat away from the grime of Tyneside. In 1869 Armstrong called on the services of Norman Shaw, a well respected architect, to transform the Estate into a grand country mansion. Over the following two decades Cragside grew to become one of the finest houses in Victorian England set in 1,700 acres of landscaped gardens with many ingenious innovations incorporated into the house and gardens; it was the first house in the world to be lit by hydro-electricity. Armstrong made his fortune through his vast manufacturing factories at Elswick along the banks of the Tyne, the development of which was largely responsible for the rapid industrial growth of Newcastle. His company became one of the most successful and innovative manufacturing businesses in the world during the late 19th Century supplying armaments, iron-clad armour for ships, guns and industrial machinery to all corners of the globe. He was created the 1st Baron Armstrong of Cragside in 1887 and by the time of his death in 1900 his company employed over 25,000 people. Cragside House and the surrounding grounds are now in the care of The National Trust, although the Armstrong family still own the remainder of the Estate including Rothbury Terraces as well as Bamburgh Castle, which Lord Armstrong acquired and completely renovated in the late 19th Century. In Rothbury itself are two groups of houses built by Lord Armstrong for retired estate workers including Addycombe Cottages (1873) and Armstrong Cottages (1896), a delightful square of twelve single-storey cottages on the outskirts of the town.

THE RIVER COQUET, pronounced 'co-cut', is claimed by many to be the finest in Northumberland, and it is easy to see why. It spans the entire breadth of the county from west to east, rising on the remote Border Ridge between Scotland and England. From its source high in the Cheviots, the Coquet begins life as a peaty burn that soon becomes a fast-flowing stream cutting a deep cleft through the lonely hills of Upper Coquetdale. At Alwinton, the river opens out from the confines of the Cheviots into a broad vale, now known as Coquetdale, its wide shallow waters meandering across pastures between wooded hillsides before skirting the feet of the Simonside Hills. At Rothbury, the valley closes in with the river channelled through a narrow gorge only a few feet wide known as The Thrum. From here, the character of the valley changes again with the river flowing through a steep-sided yet relatively shallow valley, meandering in wide loops through an undulating landscape towards Warkworth and the coastal plain. This stretch of river valley from Rothbury to the coastal plain, now known as the Coquet Valley, is a delight with a footpath charting its course for most of the way, threading through oak forest and across rich pastureland, passing beneath medieval bridges and along the riverbank itself before the final loop of the river beneath the ramparts of Warkworth Castle. *"When I walk by the Coquet I feel always that it is telling me stories. The Aln, more reticent, takes its secrets with it to bury them in the sea. Some rivers I am content to look at from above, to cross on bridges, respecting their reserve; but others call to me so that I must be down by them, looking into their bubbling shadows, dipping my hands in their deep pools. They have a tempting friendliness, but there are days when they repulse you in anger and flow past you coldly aloof."* **(Iris Wedgwood 'Northumberland and Durham' 1932.)** A feature of this walk are the many isolated farmhouses with similar suffixes; where the valley opens out enough to allow riverside pastures the farms often have the suffix 'haugh' (pronounced 'hoff'), an old Northumbrian word that means 'flat land in a valley'. Where the valley sides crowd in, then the farms have the suffix 'heugh' (pronounced 'hurf') that means 'a ridge that ends abruptly'.

PAUPERHAUGH, pronounced 'popper-hoff', is a small hamlet beside a narrow five-arch bridge in a relatively wide section of the valley at the confluence of the Coquet with Forest Burn, a tumbling stream born on the flanks of Simonside. The bridge dates from the early 19th Century and once led up to Brinkburn Station on the Rothbury Branch Line, which was several miles from Brinkburn Priory! This area formed the eastern section of the Forest of Rothbury, a Norman hunting preserve that was controlled by its own laws and privileges. The Forest was granted to Robert Fitz-Roger in 1205 by King John and later passed to the Earls of Northumberland who managed it as a deer park; vast tracts of Rothbury Forest remained as open land until it was parcelled off during the Enclosure Acts of the early 19th Century. *"A casual glance from the train as it runs through Rothbury forest does not present much to attract the notice of the stranger, but a closer acquaintance with this uninteresting looking stretch of country reveals many a poetic dell and sequestered ravine, with pleasing glimpses of woodland glades and burn-side scenery; for through the middle of the forest there extends from Moral Hurst, on the moorland slopes of Simonside, down to the river Coquet, a charming little valley in which flows the Forest Burn, its thickly wooded banks and limestone scars being covered with an endless variety of wild flowers and ferns."* **(David Dippie Dixon 1903).** As you walk down alongside the Coquet you will notice several Second World War pill-boxes, including one at Pauperhaugh. These were built in 1940 as a line of defence known as the Coquet Stop Line along the length of the river to prevent enemy penetration inland during the war.

Brinkburn Priory

BRINKBURN PRIORY, glimpsed through the trees, has a beautiful setting beside the River Coquet, surrounded by an almost complete loop of the river. It comes as little surprise that such a secluded spot has given rise to local superstitions including a story that Brinkburn is the burial place of the Northumbrian fairies! *"A shady green spot in the precincts of Brinkburn is pointed out by a pretty tradition as the burial-place of the Northumbrian fairies. Their tiny forms are no longer seen in the moon-lit glade, but the flowers they loved still bloom plentifully beneath the shelter of green groves."* **(W. W. Tomlinson 1888.)** The Priory was founded in 1135 for Augustinian Canons by William Bertram I, Baron of Mitford and was built over a forty-year period during the late 12th Century. Over the subsequent centuries, the Priory acquired various scattered pockets of land throughout the North East, however, it was never wealthy and suffered centuries of misfortune and poverty. It was a frequent target of Scottish raiders, indeed, a story is told of how on one occasion a band of Scots missed the Priory hidden away amongst the trees and were heading home when the canons decided to ring the bells as thanksgiving for not being found. Unfortunately, the Scots were out of sight but not sound and so turned back and ransacked the Priory, setting fire to it as they left! The Priory was suppressed in 1536 as part of Henry VIII's Dissolution of the Monasteries and the buildings were leased to George Fenwick, whose family held the estate until 1792. The Priory Church, dedicated to St Peter and St Paul, continued to be used as the parish church until 1683, however, it gradually fell into disrepair culminating in the collapse of the roof in the late 17th Century. The building remained almost complete, despite the loss of the roof, and so in the mid 19th Century Cadogan Hodgson Cadogan, owner of the Brinkburn estate, decided to restore the church. He employed Thomas Austin, an architect from Newcastle who had taken over the famous practice of John Dobson, and work began in 1858 to install a new roof and repair the upper masonry of the church. Contrary to many other Victorian 'restorations', this was carried out with great sympathy so that it appears contemporary with the original building. *"Then I went to look at Brinkburn, and saw that what I had heard was true. It has been restored, and now - with new buttresses, patched walls and columns, repaired mouldings, the belfry accessible by a spiral stair, and a new-tiled roof which exhibits whitewash inside between the rafters - it only waits interior fittings to be once more available as a place of worship. The ivy has been stripped from the tower, and the jackdaws, driven from their old haunt, keep up a* *perpetual remonstrance from the tops of the neighbouring trees."* **(Walter White 1859.)** Brinkburn Priory stands today as one of the finest examples of the transition from Norman to Early English architecture with a wonderful mix of pointed lancet windows combined with decorated Norman doorways. Little remains of the other monastic buildings, except for fragments of the former Refectory that were incorporated into the adjacent Manor House when it was built during the early 19th Century. The house was occupied by the Cadogan family until 1952 and is now cared for by English Heritage.

BRINKHEUGH lies just to the east of Brinkburn, a well-proportioned late 17th Century manor house that also incorporates a 16th Century bastle house. This would have provided refuge for the farmer, his family and livestock from Scottish raiders and the Border Reivers. As the Border region became more peaceful during the 17th Century, the need for defence became less important and so new, more opulent houses were built; Brinkheugh is a fine example of this transition. Just over half a mile to the east of Brinkheugh, our route crosses the line of the Roman road known as the Devil's Causeway. This road branched off from Dere Street just to the north of Hadrian's Wall and then struck a north easterly course through the heart of Northumberland to the mouth of the River Tweed.

WELDON BRIDGE is an elegant stone structure that spans the River Coquet, built in the 1760's to carry the Turnpike Road between Morpeth and Coldstream. It was probably designed by John Smeaton, a famous 18th century engineer who is often referred to as the 'first civil engineer'; some of his other more famous projects included the Eddystone Lighthouse, Forth-Clyde canal and Coldstream Bridge. During the late 18th and early 19th centuries, horse-drawn coaches would regularly cross this bridge and stop at the Anglers Arms. The coaching era was perhaps the most romantic period of travel in this country, with stagecoaches pulled by great teams of horses calling at fine roadside inns along the way. But there were dangers, for this stretch of road was a notorious haunt of highwaymen. The Anglers Arms is also a famous fisherman's pub, as the name of the pub and memorabilia inside testify, with some of the finest salmon and trout fishing on its doorstep. *"Weldon Bridge, too, further on, opens up a characteristic reach of the river, both up and down stream, and is commanded by a roomy old fishing-inn, which looks as if it might exude the post-prandial fish-stories of generations of exuberant and reminiscent anglers at every pore. But no rods rested handily against the angles of the inn walls the last time I dallied there, and the thin streams of the Coquet piped feeble airs against the buttresses of the bridge, suggestive neither of salmon nor of trout."* **(A. G. Bradley 1908.)** Such is its fame that songs and verse have been written about the inn and the fish to be had in the river:

At Weldon Bridge ther's wale o' wine,
If ye hae coin in pocket;
If ye can thraw a heckle fine,
There's wale o' trout in Coquet

There's wine in the cellar o' Weldon,
If ye ken but the turn of the key;
There are bonny, braw lassies on Coquet,
If ye ken but the blink o' their e'e.

Weldon Bridge, with its row of stone cottages climbing up the hillside, old mill and inn, is now a quiet backwater where it is quite safe to peer over the parapet without fear of speeding traffic, or highwaymen for that matter, as a 'new' bridge was constructed just downstream in 1969.

FELTON lies amidst the vast swathe of undulating countryside between the Simonside Hills and the coastal plain with only the deep gorge of the River Coquet as an obstacle. There has been a river crossing here since at least the 12th Century, although the present Felton Old Bridge dates from the 15th Century. This fine stone bridge was widened in the 18th Century - look beneath the bridge to see the original ribbed arches - and formed part of the Great North Road. Traffic was diverted away from the Old Bridge when a more modern bridge was built just downstream in the 1920's then, after years of campaigning, a by-pass was built to the west of Felton in 1981. Felton lies on the north bank of the river with an attractive row of old stone houses overlooking the historic bridge and its red telephone box. More stone cottages, an old bank building and a village 'local' line the wide main street which climbs up away from the river. To the south of the river is the hamlet of West Thirston, which boasts a fine old coaching inn, whilst just upstream is Felton Mill, one of the largest mill complexes in the county that dates from the early 19th Century; this mill was turned into housing during the 1980's. Due to its importance as a river crossing, Felton has played an important role in the history of this region. In 1215, the Northumbrian barons met up at Felton Park where they decided to transfer their allegiance from King John to King Alexander of Scotland, which led to a brutal reprisal the following year when King John ordered Felton to be burnt to the ground. Then in 1292, Edward I rode across the bridge on his way to Berwick Castle to settle the claims of the Scottish throne following the death of King Alexander of Scotland. Unfortunately, he chose John Balliol rather than Robert Bruce and then demanded recognition as the overlord of Scotland, thus sowing the seeds of three centuries of bloodshed known as the Border Troubles with the Scottish War of Independence. *"Felton, a charmingly placed little village, on the banks of the river where they are overhung by graceful woods, and diversified by cliff and grassy slope, stands just where the great North Road crosses the Coquet. By reason of this position it has been the scene of one or two events of historical interest, notably those connected with the "Fifteen" and the "Forty-five."* **(Jean F. Terry 'Northumberland, Yesterday and To-day' 1913).** During the Jacobite Rebellion of 1715, the Earl of Derwentwater and his band of supporters were joined at Felton Park by seventy Scots from just across the Border who then went on to proclaim James Stuart, the 'Old Pretender', as James III at Warkworth. This 'Fifteen Rebellion' was an attempt to restore the Catholic Stuart kings to the British throne and displace the Hanoverians, however, the Jacobite forces were defeated at Preston and the rebellion collapsed in 1716. Some thirty years later, the Jacobite forces again tried to restore the Stuart kings during the 'Forty-five Rebellion', this time Charles Stuart, the 'Young Pretender' otherwise known as Bonny Prince Charlie. After initial successes - they reached as far south as Derby - they were defeated at the Battle of Culloden in 1746; the Duke of Cumberland and his army rested at

Felton Park on their way to Culloden where they dealt the final blow to the Stuart cause. A large house and walled garden were built within Felton Park in the 18th Century, possibly on the site of an older manor house. Just above the village on the edge of Felton Park is the Church of St Michael and All Angels. This striking building dates from the early 13th Century and, at first glance, appears to be roofless due to its unusually low-pitched roof! The original church consisted of a simple broad nave, the doorway of which was incorporated into the south aisle when the church was extended in the 14th Century. The huge cave-like porch was added in the 15th Century whilst the stout bell-cote was added in the 16th Century when the roof was lowered to its present level. During restoration work in the 19th Century, seventy skulls were found in the churchyard alongside Scottish coins, the sad remains of some long forgotten battle during the Border Troubles.

BRAINSHAUGH is a small hamlet of a few cottages and the imposing Georgian Brainshaugh House, set on a wooded hillside above the River Coquet. There is evidence of farming in this area dating back several centuries with fine examples of medieval 'ridge and furrow' ploughing strips in the fields. Just beyond Waterside Cottage is the finest 18th Century weir in England, an elegant horseshoe-shaped dam with a wonderfully symmetrical cascade of water set beneath overhanging trees. Designed by Smeaton and built in 1776 to provide power for a newly-built iron foundry just downstream beside Guyzance Bridge, the weir proved quite an obstacle for some salmon to leap and was quickly blamed for the decline of the Coquet as a good salmon river, although other factors such as pollution may have played a part. When the famous naturalist Frank Buckland visited the weir a century after it was built and saw salmon trying to leap it he pinned a notice nearby that read *"NOTICE TO SALMON AND BULL TROUT! No road at present over this weir. Go down stream, taking the first turn to the right, and you will find good travelling water up stream, and no jumping required - F. T. B."* This weir has a tragic tale to tell, for in January 1945 a group of 18 year old conscripts from the 10th Duke of Wellington's Regiment and the Durham Light Infantry drowned in the flooded waters during a river crossing exercise, when their ten-man craft accidentally went over the weir. In the field adjacent to the bridge, almost surrounded by a loop of the river, are the remains of Brainshaugh Priory, also known as Guyzance Chapel. Founded in 1147 by Richard Tyson, it was given to the Premonstratensian 'White Canons' of Alnwick Abbey who then established a small nunnery here dedicated to St. Wilfred of Gysnes (hence the name of the nearby village of Guyzance). The crumbling early medieval remains of the chapel are surrounded by a high wall; marriages and services were still held within its walls up until the 18th Century. *"According to a popular tradition, there was a subterranean passage between Brainshaugh and Brinkburn. It may have been a secret footpath through the dense wood which, in early times, filled the vale of Coquet."* **(Tomlinson 1888.)**

Guyzance

GUYZANCE is a delightful village consisting of a single street lined with unpretentious single-storey stone cottages, a superb example of Northumbrian country architecture. The village was first mentioned in the 13th Century when it belonged to the Abbot of Alnwick, and stands on a flat shelf of land above the wooded slopes of the river. There are a number of notable buildings nearby including Guyzance Hall, a fine late Victorian country mansion set in splendid gardens, whilst beside the river is an overgrown and dilapidated stone-built watermill that dates from the early 19th Century. *"...still further, across the Coquet, one of the most charming of the smaller rivers of Northumberland (and one justly celebrated amongst the disciples of Izaak Walton), is the church of Guyzance, a deeply interesting ruin of a Transitional-Norman edifice, which formerly belonged to the Premonstratensian Canons of Alnwick. From beneath Guyzance the Coquet winds through a richly-wooded glen to Warkworth, seated proudly above the river and the sea, and leads the traveller to one of the most striking "bits" of the Northumbrian coast."* **(J S Fletcher 'Enchanting North' 1908.)**

WARKWORTH HERMITAGE, set in the sandstone cliffs on the north banks of the River Coquet, is one of the finest examples of a medieval hermitage in this country, offering a rare insight into the religious piety of England during the Middle Ages. For over 200 years until the Reformation this was home to a succession of hermits who were supported by the Earls of Northumberland to pray for the souls of deceased members of the Percy family. The hermits were well looked after by the Earls and received an annual stipend, pasture land, regular loads of firewood and fresh fish every Sunday! The chapel and sacristy were carved out of solid rock in the early 14th Century, and boast a fine ribbed ceiling, columns, altar and windows. Later additions to this small religious complex were made during the 15th Century including a hall, latrine and kitchen. A boat takes visitors across the river to the Hermitage during the summer months.

WARKWORTH is undeniably one of the finest towns in England, set magnificently on a wide loop in the River Coquet with a majestic castle guarding this peninsula of land from the south and a fortified bridge protecting the approach from the north. *"Warkworth must be approached from the north. With its bridge, its bridge-tower, then Bridge Street at an angle joining the main street up a hill to the towering, sharply cut block of the keep, it is one of the most exciting sequences of views one can have in England."* **(Nikolaus Pevsner 'The Buildings of England: Northumberland', 1959).** Warkworth retains its medieval layout as it was a planned borough, laid out in the 12th Century on the site of an earlier Saxon settlement, with a wide main street leading down to the market place beside the church and a 'back lane', now a footpath, running to the east behind the old burgess plots. Many of these long narrow plots of land, originally intended for livestock and vegetables, survive behind the houses along Castle Street. The borough was a valuable asset for the lord of the manor as he could raise money through market tolls, insist that his mills and ovens were used by the villagers and fine people in his feudal court. Villagers were also obliged to provide a certain amount of free labour for the lord. In return for this service, villagers enjoyed protection, employment and stability although this feudal system was quite definitely a master and servant relationship perhaps best illustrated by the large Percy lion crest on the Castle keep overlooking the town. Castle Street is a delightful tree-lined street that sweeps gracefully down from the imposing castle, lined with Georgian and Victorian houses that are built on the site of the medieval plots. The street opens out into a small market place known as Dial Place, named after the sundial on the church, surrounded by several fine Georgian houses and old inns. There is an ornate Market Cross of 1830 on an older stepped base, around which are the heraldic emblems of the Dukes of Northumberland; markets are no longer held. It was in this market place that the Old Pretender was first proclaimed King during the ill-fated Jacobite Rebellion of 1715. General Forster, the Earl of Derwentwater and forty of his followers dined in the Masons Arms on the evening of Saturday the 8th October 1715. The next morning, after his Catholic chaplain had said prayers at the church, James Stuart was proclaimed King James III. At the bottom of Dial Place is the Parish Church of St Lawrence, which was built around 1120, almost thirty years before Warkworth Castle, and stands as the most complete Norman church in Northumberland. The chancel and most of the nave, the largest in the county, are Norman. The south aisle was added in the 15th Century by the Percy family and the spire dates from the 14th Century, one of only a handful of spires in Northumberland. Inside there is a wealth of interest including a superb Norman chancel arch and a very rare stone vaulted Norman ceiling that is thought to have been constructed by the same masons that built Durham Cathedral. This church was the scene of a terrible massacre in 1174 when the Earl of Fife and his Scottish army, accompanying the Scottish King William the Lion, attacked Warkworth and murdered over 300 townsfolk who had taken refuge within the church. The large churchyard has a number of ancient and interesting gravestones including that of Edward Dodsworth, huntsman to King James I, whilst inside the church is a fine effigy of an unknown knight, known as Sir Hugh. The church actually stands on the site of a Saxon church, first mentioned in 737AD when the King of Northumbria gave it and the small Saxon village of 'Wercewode' to the monks of Lindisfarne; Werce was the name of the Abbess who gave a sheet of linen to the Venerable Bede to be used as his shroud. The foundations of this Anglo-Saxon church survive beneath the nave. A riverside path leads from the church to one of the few fortified bridges in the country. It was built in the 14th Century to replace the old ford that crossed the river near to the church. Guarded by a gatehouse at its southern end, this elegant but narrow stone structure carried all traffic into the town from the north for 600 years until it was replaced by the neighbouring steel and concrete bridge in 1965. Warkworth Castle dominates the town, its slender look-out tower visible for miles around. The soaring ramparts and towers never fail to thrill and impress with its massive angular Keep looming above the rooftops. It played an important role in the history of this turbulent Border region and was for many centuries the stronghold of the powerful Percy family - William Shakespeare set a number of scenes of his play 'Henry IV' here, although the Bard described the castle as *"...this worm eaten hold of ragged stone."* The first castle on this site was a Norman motte and bailey castle built in around 1150 by Earl Henry of Northumberland, son of King David I of Scotland, when this area formed part of the Scottish realm. Things were soon to change, however, for in 1157 King Henry II of England regained control of Warkworth and subsequently gave it to Roger FitzRichard, who rebuilt the castle in stone. Warkworth slowly grew into a magnificent defensive castle, despite several Scottish raids, and the family grew wealthy mainly due to their close connections with King John during the early 13th Century. Much building work took place during the late 12th and early 13th Century including the fine Gatehouse. However, by the early 14th Century the fortunes of the castle began to decline as the descendents of FitzRichard got into debt and so Warkworth passed back to the Crown. It was besieged twice by Scottish forces during this period, and the King soon realised that this far-off castle was too difficult to defend and so in 1332 granted it to Henry de Percy, Lord of Alnwick, a powerful family that had originated from Yorkshire but came to dominate Northumberland. Despite already owning Alnwick Castle, the Percy family spent a great deal of time at Warkworth and set about strengthening the castle's defences during the mid 14th Century with the addition of the Grey Mare's Tail Tower as well as other alterations. Then, in the late 14th Century, Henry de Percy IV, first Earl of Northumberland, built the superb Keep we see today with its towers and imposing central look-out tower, which also caught rain for drinking water. However, the first Earl became too ambitious when he, along with his son Harry Hotspur, turned against Henry IV after helping to dispose of Richard II. This ill-fated 'Rising of the Percys' led to Hotspur's death at the Battle of Shrewsbury in 1403 and Warkworth was forfeited once again to the Crown. The King tried again to rule this distant corner, but found it too difficult and so Henry V returned the castle to the Percy family, who still held great sway in this turbulent Border region. However, the fortunes of the castle had begun to wane with the Percy family falling out of favour on a number of occasions, particularly during the War of the Roses then the Gunpowder Plot and the Rising of the North in 1569, following which much of the castle was pillaged of its roofs and dressed stone. By the 17th Century, with relative peace between England and Scotland, the Earls of Northumberland neglected Warkworth in favour of Alnwick and the castle fell into disrepair. During the 19th Century the 4th Duke of Northumberland (the 1st Duke was created in 1760) undertook some restoration work, re-roofing parts of the Keep which were used for picnics during 'excursions' by the Duke and his guests from Alnwick. Warkworth Castle is now in the care of English Heritage, although it is still owned by the Duke of Northumberland.

. . . .

WARKWORTH
to
EMBLETON

✦

"The tangy smell of burning oak chippings caught my senses as I approached the Jolly Fisherman. Smoke was rising lazily from the vented roof of the smokehouse opposite, rich with the scent of autumn bonfires mixed with the sea; I knew what to order before I had even reached the bar! As I sat in the pub looking out across the harbour and the gentle swell of the steel-grey North Sea, thoughts of times past filled my mind with cobles moored along the bustling quayside and fishermen unloading their herring catch. All is now quiet around the harbour save for the occasional small boat, yet a hint of melancholy drifts in on the breeze along with the scent of sea and smoke, carrying with it memories of busier days."

Mark Reid
September 2003

WALK INFORMATION

Points of interest: The magnificent golden strands of Warkworth, Alnmouth and Embleton, a church cut off by the tide, the old grain port of Alnmouth, a smugglers' haven, Earl Grey's bathing house, superb rocky coastal path, old fishing villages, Craster kippers and the gaunt skeleton of Dunstanburgh Castle.

Distance:

Warkworth to Alnmouth	5 miles
Alnmouth to Craster	7 miles
Craster to Embleton	3 miles
Total	15 miles

Time: Allow 7 hours

Terrain: This walks follows the undulating coastal path all the way from Warkworth to Embleton along grassy tracks, across low grassy cliffs and miles of glorious golden sands. Beach walking can be tiring, especially if the sand is soft, and care must be taken during bad weather or high tides.
Please Note: The Right of Way from Foxton Hall to Seaton House heads along the beach for 0.5 miles (beneath low crumbly cliffs), which may become impassable for periods of time during certain high tides. Check tide times and plan your walk carefully (Foxton Hall is 1 mile on from Alnmouth).

Beach Access: The route has been described using Rights of Way, however, the footpath from Dunstanburgh Castle to Embleton runs behind the sand dunes, which is recommended as a 'bad weather / high tide' alternative. The best way to complete this walk is along Embleton Beach - access points and directions along the beach have been given in italics within the route description (marked by *), thus allowing you to choose your route.

NB: Please see the note on Page 13 concerning Rights of Way, Access and Beaches. The sand dune ecology is fragile - do not walk across them.

Tide Times:	See local newspapers or call the Coastguard 24-hr Information Line: 0870 6006 505
Ascents:	There are no significant ascents along this walk.
Viewpoints:	Warkworth Beach looking towards Coquet Island.
	Church Hill overlooking Alnmouth.
	Coastal path from Boulmer to Craster, particularly Howdiemont Sands, Sugar Sands, Rumbling Kern and Cullernose Point. The approach to Dunstanburgh Castle from Craster.
	Embleton Bay looking back towards Dunstanburgh Castle.

FACILITIES
. . . .

Warkworth	Inn / B&B / Shop / P.O. / Café / Bus / Phone / Toilets / Camp
Alnmouth	Inn / B&B / Shop / P.O. / Café / Bus / Train / Phone / Toilets
Boulmer	Inn / B&B / Bus / Phone / Toilets

Craster	Inn / Shop / Café / Bus / Phone / Toilets / Info / Camp
Embleton	Inn / B&B / Shop / P.O. / Café / Bus / Phone / Toilets / Camp

ROUTE DESCRIPTION

(Map Six)

From Warkworth Castle, walk down along Castle Street then head through Dial Place (Market Place) along the lane to the left of the church to reach the River Coquet. Turn right along the riverside path (SP 'Warkworth Bridge') to reach the fortified bridge. Turn left over the fortified bridge, immediately after which turn right (SP 'Beach and Warkworth Golf Club') along a lane. Follow this lane up passing the football pitch on your right then, where the road bends sharply round to the left towards the picnic site (caravan park to the right), head straight on (SP 'Warkworth Beach') through the parking area then on over sand dunes to reach Warkworth Beach. Turn left along the beach for about 0.75 miles then, as you approach the rocky outcrops of Birling Carrs, turn left up along a small inlet / gap in the dunes (lifebelt and a wooden bridge across the inlet). Head up this inlet, passing beneath the bridge up across the golf course (take care - beware of golf balls) to quickly reach a gate and onto a track. Turn right along the track and follow it on bending to the right (across the golf course again - take care) then left into a caravan park. Follow the clear track through the caravan site then, where Alnmouth Bay comes into view, keep to the clear track bending to the left then down to the right to reach a FB (National Trust sign 'Alnmouth Dunes') at the end of the caravan site. Head straight on over the FB along the clear path up through bracken across the dunes to run alongside a stone wall on your left, which you follow on heading towards Alnmouth in the distance. The path drops down and becomes a clearer track that leads on through a gate across your path, after which carry straight on (track now a gravel road) passing parking areas on your right and a large ruined stone barn on your left then follow the track curving round to the left (Church Hill short detour straight on at this bend) up to join the main road (A1068). As you reach the main road turn right along the roadside footpath / cycleway (SP 'Alnmouth'). Follow this clear roadside path on passing the turning towards Waterside House then continue straight on along the roadside path for a further 0.75 miles then follow it as it turns sharp right (heading towards Duchess Bridge in the distance) then round to the left on to reach the road (B1338). Turn right along the road, over Duchess Bridge across the River Aln immediately after which turn right down some steps beside the bridge (SP 'Lovers Walk') onto a riverside path. Follow this path on with the estuary on your right then heading to the left passing a play area on to join a lane (Garden Terrace) which you follow to the left up into Alnmouth.

(Map Seven)

As you emerge onto the main street (Northumberland Street), turn left passing the Church then turn right along The Wynd (old drinking fountain on the corner). Follow this road down then, where it bends to the right, take the turning to the left (sign 'Parking') across Alnmouth Common (playing fields and golf course to your right). Follow this lane down then turn left just after the ornate drinking fountain across a small parking area (SP 'Foxton Hall, Boulmer'). Head along the left-hand grassy path (running parallel to the clearer track) that climbs up the bank, passing some Second World War concrete blocks (painted as dice) up onto the top of the bank where the path levels out (beside an old pillbox). Head straight on along the top of the ridge along the clear wide track, which soon becomes a footpath that leads on alongside the fence on your left down across the golf course then, at the end of the golf course, carry straight on up a small bank to reach a small gate (waymarker) with the sea down to your right. Follow the clear coastal path straight on along the top of a small bank (sea to your right, golf course to your left) then, where the path divides as you approach the club house (markerpost - the permissive path to the right is a short-cut to the beach), bear left along the clearly marked path to join a metalled lane just to the left of the clubhouse. Turn right along the lane (clubhouse on your right) then as you reach the small parking area to the side of the clubhouse, follow the path on the left-side of the wall down along the edge of the golf course to join a clear track that leads down to the beach. Turn left along the beach for 0.5 miles beneath low crumbly cliffs to reach some concrete steps at Seaton Point. (NB: This short section may become impassable for periods of time during certain high tides.) At the top of the steps turn right (SP 'Boulmer') along the cliff-top path passing some seaside huts on to quickly reach a rough track where you turn left to reach a gravel track at Seaton House. Turn right along the track and follow it into Seaton Point Caravan Site then, where the track divides, follow the left-hand track alongside the fence on your left heading along the edge of the caravan site then bending round to the left to reach a gate at the end of the site. Head straight on along the clear coastal path to reach a kissing gate to your right beside the two large navigational posts. After the gate, turn left across the beach then up onto the road at Boulmer opposite the Lifeboat Station (Boulmer Volunteer Rescue Service). Turn right along the road through the village passing the Fishing Boat Inn then, where the road turns sharply to the left, continue straight on (SP 'Boulmer Steel'). This road soon becomes a track, which you follow straight on for 0.5 miles (along the coast) to reach a bridle-gate that leads over a FB (on the beach) then through another bridle-gate back onto the grassy track. Continue along the grassy track which leads on over the parking area for Howdiemonth Sands (ignore the lane to the left), after which carry straight on along the track (SP 'Craster') climbing up slightly then levelling out (Sugar Sands down to your right) before dropping down to reach a large FB across Howick Burn. Just after this FB, take the path to the right off this track over a stile (by the two stone gateposts). The clear coastal path leads on through gorse and trees then emerges to run along a grassy bank with the rocky foreshore to your right, passing below Sea Houses Farm with the sea-carved outcrops of Rumbling Kern on your right on to join a lane near to the Bathing House (stone house) perched on the edge of the rocky coastline.

Head straight on (SP 'Coastal Path Craster') passing the Bathing House along the very clear coastal path, which runs alongside the road for a while then continues on following the coastline before climbing up onto the cliffs of Cullernose Point (seabird nesting site). Follow the path bending to the right across the top of the cliffs (take care) then round to the left along the grassy coastal path once again heading towards Craster. As you approach the houses, the path skirts to the left around the inlet of Hole o' the Dike then, at the top of this inlet, the path splits - head right through a gate just to the right of the houses. Follow the clear coastal path straight on into Craster, passing through a play area (keep to the coastal path) and on through the beer garden of the Jolly Fisherman to join a lane beside the south Harbour Wall. Head left along this track to quickly reach the road (pub on your left), where you turn right down through Craster skirting to the right around the Harbour along Dunstanburgh Road (SP 'Dunstanburgh Castle') that leads on to a gate and the coastal footpath. A clear path leads straight on with the rocky coastline on your right all the way to Dunstanburgh Castle. As you approach the castle, a grassy path branches off to the left after a gate - follow this left-hand path passing beneath rocky outcrops (boggy ground - site of old moat) then beneath the castle ramparts. Follow the path as it bears round to the right beneath Lilburn Tower on to reach the coastline again and a gate at Dunstanburgh Castle Golf Course. *(Beach Route from this point *)*. After this gate (beside the golf green) the path divides, head left along the clear gravel path which runs along the fence on your left (be aware of golfers and golf balls). Follow this fence-line straight on along the edge of the golf course (soon becomes grassy path), passing the end of a lane at Dunstan Steads, and continue on alongside the fence / hedge along the edge of the Golf Course then, as you approach the Club House, head over a FB on to reach the bottom of the lane beside the Club House. Follow this lane up into Embleton.

* Beach Route - Dunstanburgh Castle to Embleton: *After the gate that leads onto the Golf Course, where the path divides (beside the golf green) follow the track to the right, with the golf course on your left and the rocky foreshore on* *your right, passing a pillbox then continue on over low sand dunes (keep to the clear path) and drop down to reach the southern end of the sands of Embleton Bay. Walk northwards along the beach for about 0.5 miles then, just before you reach Embleton Burn that cuts through a break in the sand dunes, head left along the clear path through the dunes, over a FB across the burn then up across the Golf Course to join the bottom of a lane beside the Club House. Follow this lane up into Embleton.*

Alnmouth

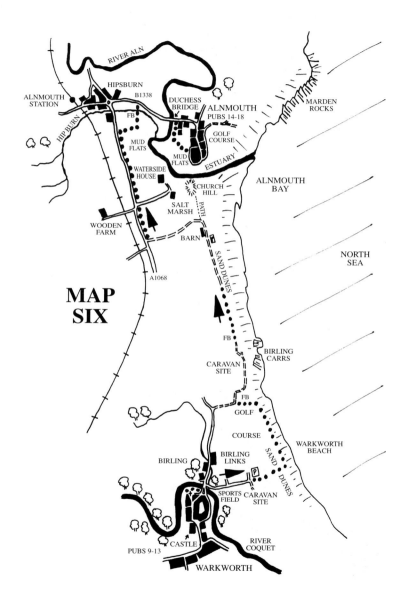

MAP
SIX

RIVER ALN

ALNMOUTH
STATION

HIPSBURN

B1338

HIP BURN

FB

DUCHESS
BRIDGE

ALNMOUTH
PUBS 14-18

MUD
FLATS

MUD
FLATS

GOLF
COURSE

ESTUARY

MARDEN
ROCKS

WATERSIDE
HOUSE

CHURCH
HILL

ALNMOUTH
BAY

SALT
MARSH

PATH

WOODEN
FARM

BARN

A1068

SAND DUNES

NORTH
SEA

FB

CARAVAN
SITE

BIRLING
CARRS

FB

GOLF

COURSE

WARKWORTH
BEACH

BIRLING

BIRLING
LINKS

SAND DUNES

P

SPORTS
FIELD

CARAVAN
SITE

CASTLE

PUBS 9-13

RIVER
COQUET

WARKWORTH

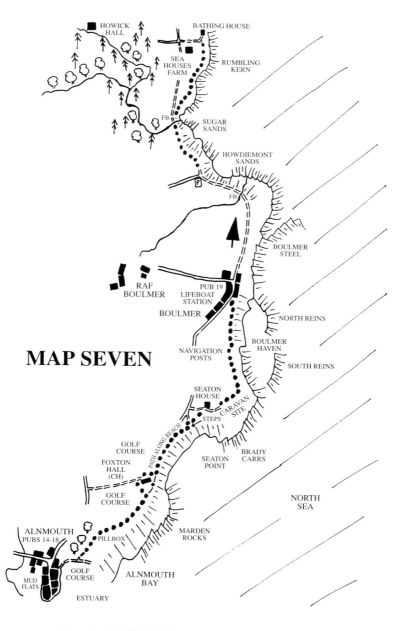

MAP SEVEN

HOWICK HALL
BATHING HOUSE
SEA HOUSES FARM
RUMBLING KERN
FB
SUGAR SANDS
HOWDIEMONT SANDS
P
FB
BOULMER STEEL
RAF BOULMER
PUB 19 LIFEBOAT STATION
BOULMER
NORTH REINS
NAVIGATION POSTS
BOULMER HAVEN
SOUTH REINS
SEATON HOUSE
CARAVAN SITE
STEPS
GOLF COURSE
PATH ALONG BEACH
SEATON POINT
BRADY CARRS
NORTH SEA
FOXTON HALL (CH)
GOLF COURSE
ALNMOUTH
PUBS 14-18
PILLBOX
MARDEN ROCKS
GOLF COURSE
MUD FLATS
ALNMOUTH BAY
ESTUARY

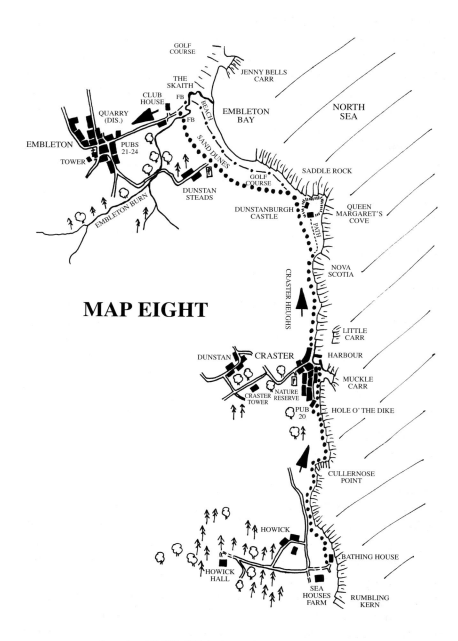

MAP EIGHT

GOLF
COURSE

JENNY BELLS
CARR

THE
SKAITH

CLUB
HOUSE

FB

QUARRY
(DIS.)

EMBLETON
BAY

NORTH
SEA

BEACH

SAND DUNES

EMBLETON

PUBS
21-24

TOWER

FB

GOLF
COURSE

SADDLE ROCK

EMBLETON BURN

DUNSTAN
STEADS

DUNSTANBURGH
CASTLE

QUEEN
MARGARET'S
COVE

PATH

NOVA
SCOTIA

CRASTER HEUGHS

LITTLE
CARR

DUNSTAN

CRASTER

HARBOUR

MUCKLE
CARR

CRASTER
TOWER

NATURE
RESERVE

PUB
20

HOLE O' THE DIKE

CULLERNOSE
POINT

HOWICK

BATHING HOUSE

HOWICK
HALL

SEA
HOUSES
FARM

RUMBLING
KERN

WARKWORTH BEACH is a fine, gently curving dune-backed beach that, rather surprisingly, is littered with pieces of coal. Across to the right are the large breakwaters of Amble Harbour, which was once a busy fishing port during the 19th and early 20th Centuries from where coal was also shipped out from the many collieries and open cast mines along this stretch of the Northumberland coastline; this coal trade came to an end over thirty years ago and the old coal ships, staithes and jetties have been replaced by a large marina. The coal seams run out under the North Sea fairly close to the seabed, hence the numerous pieces of fossil fuel on the beach. Up until 1765, the River Coquet made one last loop before entering the sea, however, a storm changed the course of the river to a more direct route - the original mouth of the Coquet was roughly where our footpath leads over the dunes to the beach. The old estuary was known as Warkworth Harbour and was used by small fishing boats as far back as the 14th Century. Further out to sea beyond Amble is Coquet Island, now a nature reserve and bird sanctuary. This island was formerly an important monastic site, settled by monks as far back as the 7th Century. The remains of medieval monastic buildings, built by monks from Tynemouth Priory, have been incorporated into the 19th Century lighthouse; one of its keepers was William Darling, brother of the famous heroine Grace Darling. The whole coastline from Amble to Berwick is protected as an Area of Outstanding Natural Beauty, known as the Northumberland Heritage Coast.

ALNMOUTH is situated on a peninsula of land at the mouth of the River Aln (pronounced 'allun') surrounded on three sides by water. The river cuts a wide channel to the west and south of the town, providing safe mooring for small boats. This river channel separates the town from Church Hill, a small grassy hill immediately to the south of Alnmouth; a bridleway is shown on the map fording this estuary, however, the soft sand and fast flowing tidal river make for a hazardous crossing, tempting though it is as the walk round to Alnmouth, which is only a stone's throw away from Church Hill, takes an hour! Church Hill, with its large wooden cross, provides the best viewpoint across the estuary towards the red roof tiles of the town clustered on the peninsula. It was the site of the Anglo-Saxon settlement of Twyford, or 'two fords', where

St Cuthbert was chosen to be Bishop of Lindisfarne in 684 at the Synod of Twyford in the presence of the King of Northumbria. Fragments of a 10th Century inscribed Saxon cross were found on Church Hill in 1789 indicating that this has been a place of worship for over 1,000 years. The town we see today was founded by William de Vescy, Lord of Alnwick, in the mid 12th Century as the port for Alnwick and was one of the first Norman 'new towns' in Northumberland following the Conquest; Alnmouth was very privileged as it was granted 'borough' status. This new town required a suitable place of worship to reflect its status and so the old Saxon church was replaced by a larger stone-built Norman church, dedicated to St Waleric; at this time, Church Hill was connected to the town by a strip of land with the River Aln flowing to the south of the hill. The planned town consisted of houses running along a main street with burgage plots behind, the layout of which remains very much intact. It quickly prospered as a thriving fishing and commercial port especially during the 13th and 14th Centuries, indeed during this period the ships of Alnmouth were required for the defence of England in times of conflict. After a slight lull in its fortunes, Alnmouth enjoyed its most prosperous period during the 18th Century when it became one of the most important ports in the North for the export of corn and grain as well as imports of timber from Scandinavia and other European goods. It also became a rather surreptitious centre for smuggling; when John Wesley visited the town in 1748 to preach he commented that it was… *"A small seaport town famous for all kinds of wickedness."* Picture the scene with dozens of sloops and schooners sailing into and out of the estuary, the quayside bustling with sailors and fishermen and cartloads of grain clattering across the cobbles down from one of the dozen or so large granaries along the main street. Alnmouth became such an important port that a Corn Road was built to it from Hexham in the Tyne Valley in the 1750's; the town's wealth of fine buildings and houses date from this period of great prosperity. According to local tradition, John Paul Jones, an American naval officer, fired at Alnmouth in 1779 as he sailed south prior to the Battle of Flamborough Head. Jones, who was actually Scottish, became a hero during the American War of Independence when he performed several daring exploits off the British coast sinking ships and attacking ports. Fortunately, he was not such a good shot and his cannonballs whistled past Church Hill and hit a nearby farmhouse instead! A terrible storm on Christmas Day in 1806 did much more damage when strong winds and lashing rain changed the course of the river, cutting a new channel immediately to the north of Church Hill separating it from the town which it served. The old harbour began to silt up and the new river channel undercut Church Hill causing the Norman church to collapse, although it had been in a bad state repair for many years. The new estuary was not deep enough for many ships and so the port set into a steady decline, accelerated by the arrival of the railway in 1850; the last merchant ship sailed out of Alnmouth in 1896. The railway may have taken trade from the port of Alnmouth, but it also brought visitors and tourists from the burgeoning towns and cities of the North East who wanted to get away from the grime of the city and take in the sea air and fine beaches. Several large Victorian and Edwardian villas were built overlooking the estuary to cater for these wealthy tourists. The Duchess of Northumberland arranged for a new bridge to be built across the River Aln to provide a direct route from the town to the new Railway Station; this bridge opened in 1864 and is known as Duchess Bridge. *"On that larger and altogether more attractive half of the Northumbrian coast, stretching northward from Warkworth and Alnmouth, there are several villages which have quite recently awoke to find themselves, if not famous, at any rate much sought after by holiday-makers, and scarcely able to keep pace with the modest tide of their waxing popularity. For, save at Alnmouth, where two or three terraces of Victorian villas suggest, at any rate, his blighting finger at the edge of a not unpicturesque townlet, the jerry-builder appears to have gained but scant footing on this coast."* **(A. G. Bradley 'The Romance of Northumberland' 1908)** Northumberland Street sweeps gracefully up from the mouth of the estuary to the War Memorial, and is lined with a number of 18th and 19th Century buildings including several old granaries. Just beside the Church of St John the Baptist, which was built in 1876 by the Duke of Northumberland to replace the old church that was destroyed by the storm, is the finest example of one of these old granaries, now used as the Post Office. Just down from here is the Village Grill Gift and Coffee Shop, easily identifiable by its small balcony and protruding façade, which was originally the Custom Officer's House that dates back to the 1750's. At the top of Northumberland Street set high above The Wynd with fine views across the town is the Friary of St Francis, which was originally built in the early 20th Century for a wealthy ship-owner from Newcastle. Other buildings of note include Grosvenor Terrace, another granary building that was converted into housing in the 19th Century, to the side of which is a lane that leads down to Lovaine Terrace, a row of brightly painted houses that overlook the river, built in around 1860 by the Duke of Northumberland using concrete blocks, some of the earliest concrete houses in the country. The real highlight of Alnmouth is its beaches, coastline and estuary. The old silted up harbour and river mouth to the south of Church Hill is now an expansive area of salt marsh, mud flats and sand dunes that form one of the most important salt-marsh meadows in Northern England. Just across the mud flats to the side of Church Hill are the roofless remains of a small Mortuary Chapel that was built in 1870, despite its Norman appearance, as part of a failed plan to re-open the old churchyard beside Church Hill. To the north of the estuary a fine beach stretches northwards backed by Alnmouth Common, a large swathe of open parkland that is home to one of the oldest golf courses in the country that was founded in 1869 as well as two 19th Century lifeboat houses. Situated on the grassy bank above the Common, with far-reaching views across the bay, is an old battery that was built by the Duke of Northumberland for the use of the Percy Artillery Volunteers in 1881, a rare early example of a gun emplacement that was later modified and adapted during the Second World War as part of the coastal defences.

BOULMER, pronounced 'boomer', is a traditional Northumbrian fishing village with old stone cottages looking out to sea, fishing boats pulled up onto the undulating sandy green and lobster pots stacked against rusting tractors, with the sound of seabirds all around and the tangy smell of sea-spray in the air. The natural harbour of Boulmer Haven, formed by the gently shelving fingers of rock known as North and South Reins, has provided safe anchorage for boats for centuries;

large navigational posts guide boats through the narrow opening in these rocks into the broad bay. A handful of traditional 'cobles' are often pulled up onto the slipway opposite the old RNLI Lifeboat Station, which was established in the village in 1825 but controversially withdrawn in 1968. However, local people believed that a rescue service was still needed so they set up their own Boulmer Volunteer Rescue Service! Take a closer look at the design of the cobles with their distinctive sharp prows to cut through high waves and wide, shallow hulls for stability, which is thought to date back to the Viking long-ships. Boulmer was once notorious for smuggling with people coming from all across the North East to pick up barrels of illicit contraband including tobacco, gin, brandy and rum brought from the continent on 'rum runners'. During the 18th and 19th Centuries, high taxes on imported luxury goods, coupled with Boulmer's isolated location, meant that smuggling became a lucrative occupation - it soon became the smuggling capital of Northumberland with most of the village involved to a greater or lesser degree, although penalties were severe for those unfortunate enough to be caught by the Excise Officers. The Fishing Boat Inn was once a favourite haunt of smugglers, and it is said that many of the old cottages in the village had hiding places where liquor was stored - stories are told of barrels of rum being accidentally dug up on the beach many years after the smuggling trade had died out, so keep your eyes peeled! Nearby is RAF Boulmer, where two yellow Sea King helicopters are based, part of the Air Sea Search and Rescue. *"The coast north of Alnmouth becomes rocky and wild, and very picturesque, and the villages along the coast are being sought out by holiday makers in increasing numbers, year by year. Boulmer, one of these villages, was a famous place for smuggling in the old days, and many an exciting scene and sharp encounter took place between the smugglers and the King's men."* **(Jean F. Terry 'Northumberland, Yesterday and To-day' 1913).** The coastline from Boulmer all the way to Craster is an absolute delight with small coves, golden beaches, rocky foreshores and Dunstanburgh Castle set magnificently on a headland in the distance. Of particular note are Howdiemont Sands and Sugar Sands, beyond which the coastline becomes much more dramatic with the bare bones of the land exposed on the foreshore with wave-cut cliffs, coves and rock pools including the superb Rumbling Kern just below Sea Houses Farm, a large wave-cut 'blow hole' through which the sea surges into a pool.

Boulmer

THE BATHING HOUSE, with its distinctive chimney pots, stands rather precariously on the edge of wave-pounded cliffs, originally built as a cottage in the 18th Century then altered in about 1840 by the 2nd Earl Grey of nearby Howick Hall as a bathing house and changing rooms for his extensive family of sixteen children! Steps were cut in the rock down to a pool that was used to bathe in seawater. Howick Hall stands a mile or so inland surrounded by extensive colourful gardens and has been the home of the Grey family since 1319; the present house was built in 1782 to replace an older 15th Century pele tower. This was the home of Charles, 2nd Earl Grey, the 'great reformer' who, as Prime Minister in 1832, passed the controversial Reform Bill that both extended voting rights and altered parliamentary constituencies, which helped create the electoral system we have today. He is perhaps best known for his taste in tea! When he was Prime Minister, Earl Grey sent an envoy over to China who, according to folklore, then saved the life of a Mandarin. The grateful Mandarin in return sent back a special blend of tea flavoured with bergamot oil. Earl Grey liked this tea so much that he asked his Newcastle based tea merchants, Twinings, to recreate it for him and so from then on people would ask for Earl Grey's tea blend. From the Bathing House, a narrow footpath strikes north along the coast to reach Cullernose Point, an outcrop of Whin Sill cliffs that juts into the sea, providing the perfect nesting site for hundreds of noisy sea birds. This dramatic intrusion of dolerite rock was formed by volcanic activity some 280 million years ago when this extremely hard igneous rock pushed up between existing strata, resulting in great columns of rock reminiscent of the Giant's Causeway. The Great Whin Sill can be traced right across the county from Lindisfarne down along the coast to Cullernose Point before striking south west appearing as a long ridge of crags above the Tyne Valley, so skilfully utilised by Roman engineers when they were building Hadrian's Wall. As it is harder than the surrounding rocks, it has weathered more slowly producing a hard ridge of rock prefect for castles such as Bamburgh and Dunstanburgh.

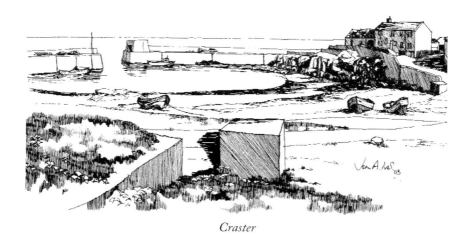

Craster

CRASTER is a delightful fishing village with a jumble of old fishermen's cottages crowded around a small harbour, complete with a small RNLI Lifeboat Station, where a handful of fishing boats are often moored with stacks of lobster pots dotted around the quayside. It developed as a fishing village in the small natural harbour formed by the outlying rocks of Little Carr and Muckle Carr, although the medieval village of Craster was actually situated around Craster Tower just to the west of the harbour. The Craster family have held the manor since 1272, although their pele tower dates from the early 15th Century built in response to the threat from Scottish raiders. By the 18th Century such threats had subsided so they built a splendid Georgian house adjoining their old tower. Between the harbour and Craster Tower is a low ridge of whinstone known as Craster Heughs on which are the remains of an ancient settlement, indeed the old name for Craster is 'Craucestr' which means the 'fort of the crows'; the Craster family coat of arms incorporates a crow. *"The two hundred or so individuals who occupy this eminently picturesque and wave-washed hamlet, like those of others on the coast, have no traffic to speak of with the hinds and bondagers and day-labourers who till the large farms that lie behind. They neither marry nor are given in marriage with them. Even their rendering of the Northumbrian speech is slightly different, and is pitched in a somewhat softer key. Their isolation from the landsman is tolerably complete till they make their final voyage to the distant cemetery of Embleton, which has succeeded the crowded churchyard, where farmer and quarryman, fisherman and hind, have at length to dispense with time-honoured cleavages and all lie down together."* **(A. G. Bradley 1908)** By the 18th Century the village beside Craster Tower had all but disappeared in favour of the developing fishing village. It was not until the 19th Century that the fishing industry took off on a commercial scale, especially as the taste for smoked herrings, known locally as kippers, grew in popularity. At its height before the First World War, a score of herring boats worked out of the harbour with four herring yards in Craster itself. During the herring season from May to September, great shoals would steadily move south from Scotland down along the coast followed by a transitional workforce of fishermen and Scottish 'herring girls' who could split and gut 2,000 herring a day! These Scottish fishwives would live in run-down buildings above the herring sheds called kipper or 'kip' houses, hence they went off to have a kip! The herring catches were landed and then either salted in one of the herring yards for export to Russia and Germany, sent fresh to

Billingsgate Market or 'kippered' to preserve the fish for the winter months. By the 1930's, the herring fishing industry along the Northumbrian coast was in terminal decline due to competition from larger trawlers coupled with dwindling stocks. A handful of small boats still work out of Craster, bringing in catches of crabs, lobster and salmon; the herrings are now imported from Scotland. The small harbour at Craster was built in 1906 in memory of Captain John Charles Craster of the 46th Punjabis who fell in action during the Tibetan Expedition of June 1904; his family decided to construct this rather unusual memorial to him as he had always shown an interest in building a harbour at Craster. It developed into a busy little place exporting whinstone from the local quarries, which helped offset the impact of the declining fishing industry. High quality stone was extracted from quarries along Craster Heughs and then transported to the harbour where the stone was loaded into waiting boats ready to be shipped throughout the country for road-building and to cities such as London where it was used as kerbstones; the base of the large concrete silos used to store the whinstone can still be seen at the end of the pier. The quarry closed in 1939, its floor now used as the main car park for the village whilst other areas of the quarry, extending across Craster Heughs, were quickly colonised by trees and plants and now form an important haven for wildlife. It is protected as a Nature Reserve, dedicated to Dr Lawrence Arnold, one of the founder members of the Northumberland Wildlife Trust. There is still a working smokehouse in the village, situated across the road from the Jolly Fisherman Inn, where they produce the famous Craster kippers. L. Robson & Sons is the fourth generation of a family business that still make traditional oak-smoked kippers in a smokehouse that was built in 1856. The smell of the delicately fragranced wood smoke drifting from the eaves of the smokehouse across the rooftops of Craster is one of the highlights of this walk, only to be topped by actually eating some kippers for breakfast! The coastal path northwards from Craster is superb, with the gaunt skeleton of Dunstanburgh Castle in the distance. Just off the path up to the left hidden away on Craster Heughs is one of the first radar stations in the world, built during the Second World War as part of the Chain Home Low system along the east coast, a top secret experimental radar system that could detect enemy aircraft approaching; this new radar system helped changed the course of the war. There are also a number of concrete pillboxes along this coastline built to protect the gently shelving beaches.

DUNSTANBURGH CASTLE stands silhouetted against the skyline, one of the most dramatic and evocative ruins in the British Isles with its gaunt towers rising up from a large rocky outcrop of volcanic dolerite rock. It was in 1313 that Thomas, Earl of Lancaster, ordered a castle to be built on this strategic peninsula on land given to his father by Henry III in 1269; the castle was largely complete after only three years. But why he chose this remote windswept spot has remained somewhat of a mystery. Thomas was the cousin of Edward II and second only to the King in terms of wealth and power; he was also his arch-rival. Edward II was thought by many to be incompetent both politically and militarily, taking too much guidance from his 'favourites' including Piers Gaveston, widely believed to be his lover. The King had to contend with disgruntled lords and barons who often challenged his power, indeed, the Earl of Lancaster was the leader of these rebellious barons and was constantly undermining the king, becoming at one stage virtual ruler of the country under the title High Steward of England, although he was disliked almost as much as the King. In 1312 the barons, under the direction of the Earl of Lancaster, seized Gaveston and executed him. This led to conflict between them both, which culminated in the capture of the Earl of Lancaster at the Battle of Boroughbridge in 1322 and his execution for treason. This perhaps explains why this castle was built as he may have feared reprisals following the death of Gaveston, not to mention the heightened threat from the Scots who had begun to launch cross-border attacks due to the ineffectual leadership of Edward II, but perhaps it was a bold statement of power in this troubled Border region that said the Earl of Lancaster was in charge - Dunstanburgh Castle was built on a grand scale to reflect the importance of its owner. *"To my mind there is something infinitely tragic, infinitely beautiful about Dunstanburgh as it stands to-day. Vast and shattered, it still reigns over that lonely countryside, a very emblem of human frailty and human magnificence. An emblem also, a significant emblem of the* *domestic architecture of a day when the price of ambition was doubt and insecurity, when the successful man's home had in truth to be his castle."* **(Iris Wedgwood 'Northumberland and Durham' 1932).** Following the death of the Earl of Lancaster, the castle passed to his heirs then in the 1380's it passed through marriage to John of Gaunt, third son of Edward III, who became the Duke of Lancaster and lord of Dunstanburgh; he was so wealthy that he even had his own tax bracket! He extended the castle, in response to the continued threat from the Scots, with the addition of a new gatehouse and turned the original gatehouse into the keep. When his son became Henry IV, Dunstanburgh became a Royal castle controlled by Constables. During the Wars of the Roses in the 15th Century it became a stronghold of the Lancastrian forces, but was besieged by Richard Neville 'the Kingmaker', Earl of Warwick, and fell to the Yorkist forces. Sadly, such a grand castle was left to fall into ruin predominantly due to its lack of military importance, then in 1604 the castle was sold by the Crown into private hands. During this turbulent period it is said that Queen Margaret, wife of the Lancastrian King Henry VI, sheltered within the castle during a siege before escaping by boat from a small inlet below the cliffs on its eastern side still known as Queen Margaret's Cove. Despite its crumbling appearance, the remains are still impressive with the shattered pinnacles of the magnificent gatehouse built by Thomas, Earl of Lancaster rising high above the headland. Much of the curtain wall still encloses the castle site, which at eleven acres is the largest castle in Northumberland, although the north wall has crumbled away leaving precipitous cliffs high above the pounding sea. On its north western side stands the gaunt ruins of Lilburn Tower, built by Sir John Lilburn in 1325 as a watchtower when he became Constable of the Castle. When the castle was built there would have been a ring of outer defences beyond the stone walls consisting of a wooden palisade and large freshwater moat known as the Great Ditch on its more vulnerable western side; the site of this moat can still be discerned as an area of boggy ground at the bottom of the slope. There was also a harbour here in the small bay of Nova Scotia just to the south of the Gatehouse, where a fleet of Henry VIII's warships sheltered in 1514 - some historians suggest that the original Gatehouse was built to impress visitors arriving by ship from this harbour. Over the centuries, the harbour has silted up and become in-filled with boulders washed south from the crags around the castle. Dunstanburgh Castle is reputedly haunted by a knight, Sir Guy the Seeker. One stormy night, Sir Guy lost his way and sought shelter in the castle ruins, however, as he walked into the grounds he saw the ghostly figure of a wizard who led him into a room beneath the castle where an enchanted princess lay asleep, held captive by several sleeping knights and their horses. The ghostly figure told Sir Guy that, in order to wake her and set her free, he had to choose either a horn or a sword that had been placed on the sleeping princess. Unfortunately, he chose the horn, which he blew and woke up all the knights instead! Sir Guy fainted with fear and awoke to find himself lying outside the gatehouse, unable to find the secret chamber nor the princess. It is said that Sir Guy still roams the castle searching for the enchanted princess, asking anyone who will listen where he may find her.

Dunstanburgh Castle

EMBLETON BAY sweeps northwards from Dunstanburgh Castle towards Newton Point below which is the hidden village of Low Newton-by-the-Sea. This is undeniably one of the finest beaches along the beautiful Northumberland coastline with soft golden sands backed by high dunes and impressive views back towards the castle. Of particular interest is the Saddle Rock, a swirl of hardened lava near where the footpath first meets the rocky foreshore to the north of the castle. This whole stretch of beach is thankfully in the care of The National Trust, although the Dunstanburgh Castle Golf Club occupies the grassy 'links' to the west of the sand dunes. But this is not just any old golf course as it was founded in 1900 and laid out by the famous golf course designer and championship golfer James Braid, the first golfer to win five Open championships, who designed over two hundred courses throughout the British Isles including the famous King's Course at Gleneagles.

EMBLETON is an attractive village of old cottages, houses and pubs set around a small pleasant green on the lee-ward side of a gently rising ridge of the Great Whin Sill. This shelters the village from the worst of the North Sea winds and provides a superb panorama of Embleton Bay as well as views of the Cheviot Hills in the far distance, as the street-name testifies! This whinstone ridge was quite extensively quarried for about 100 years until the quarry closed in 1961; it is said that the Mersey Tunnel was paved with setts from Embleton Quarry. Embleton was first mentioned in the 12th Century when it was the centre of the barony of Embleton, which passed through several hands before being granted to Edmund, Earl of Lancaster by his father Henry III in 1269. Through marriage this passed to John of Gaunt in 1362 and it remained Crown property until it was sold to Sir Ralph Grey of Chillingham Castle in 1604. During medieval times, Embleton was a thriving place with a weekly market, annual fair and farmers, millers, a blacksmith and, most importantly, a brewer living in the village. In addition to the humble dwellings of the village folk, there were a number of important medieval buildings including the Moot Hall, Church, Vicar's Pele and a lepers' hospital. No trace remains of this hospital, though a house along Station Road stands on the site of the medieval Moot Hall where manorial courts were once held. The glory of Embleton is Holy Trinity Church, with its unusual chancel and nave alignment that are set at slight angles to each other, possibly indicating an earlier Saxon church. At first glance the church appears to have suffered at the hands of Victorian 'restorers', however, its history becomes apparent upon entering the building. The original 12th Century church was extended during the 13th to 15th Centuries with the addition of aisles and a larger tower, although the base of the tower is Norman. The arches flanking the nave boast striking dog-tooth mouldings and pointed arches, a fine example of Transitional architecture dating from around 1200. The church was 'restored' in 1850 by John Dobson, the famous architect from Newcastle, and then again in 1867 when the chancel was rebuilt. Inside the church are memorials to the Craster family and also the Grey family of Fallodon, the most famous of whom was Viscount Edward Grey of Fallodon, relative of the Greys of Howick, British Foreign Secretary from 1905 to 1916 who famously said *"The lamps are going out all over Europe; we shall not see them lit again in our lifetime."* Beside the church is a fine example of a defensive tower house known as the Vicar's Pele, built in the 14th Century when an existing manor house was fortified against the growing threat from across the Border. As this threat diminished, the three-storey tower was incorporated into a larger mock-Tudor house designed by John Dobson in 1828. This former vicarage is private but can easily be seen from the churchyard. *"Happy is the parish which keeps its church in repair as here at Embleton; the vicarage, with its embrasures and solid weatherbeaten walls, looks as if it had once been a fortress. The tombstones and inscriptions are mostly in full mourning, both alike black, whereby much of the effect of epitaphs is lost."* (**Walter White 'Northumberland and The Border' 1859**). Embleton today is a quiet village away from the busier tourist honey-pots along the coast. Overlooking the small triangular green, with its old water-pump and drinking fountain built to commemorate the coronation of their 'Gracious Majesties King George V and Queen Mary' in 1911, is the Old Manse where the world-famous journalist William T. Stead was born in 1849, son of a minister who preached at the neighbouring Presbyterian Chapel. Stead was a famous and renowned journalist who became Editor of The Northern Echo then the Pall Mall Gazette. He was the outspoken champion of good causes including social justice, equality and morality as well as, quite controversially at that time, women's emancipation and anti-prostitution. Through his use of headlines, interviews and illustrations he revolutionised journalism setting the benchmark for the tabloid journalism of today. Sadly, he died on the Titanic.

STAGE THREE

EMBLETON
to
BAMBURGH

✦

"A spring breeze lifted the swell of the sea into small white crests, with waves occasionally catching the rocks of the Farne Islands sending spray high up into the air. A collection of brightly painted booths around the harbour tempted me to buy a ticket for a 2-hour 'cruise' around the Farne Islands, a wonderful collection of small rocky islands just off the Northumbrian coast that provide some of the best breeding grounds in this country for seabirds and seals. We chugged out of the harbour in an old fishing boat and soon hit open sea, rolling and pitching our way out to the farthest island of Longstone with its famous lighthouse. The strong and unmistakable smell of guano caught my throat as we approached a squawking colony of kittiwakes on Staple Island, before reaching terra firma on Inner Farne. This is a truly spiritual place where St Cuthbert found peace and solace, and where he spent his final days. A place of pilgrimage and Christian worship for centuries, the island is now an important breeding ground for seabirds, including fulmars, cormorants, shags, eiders, gulls, terns and auks. Perhaps the most striking feature of the island are the many hundreds of small burrows that pepper the ground, the nesting sites of the brightly coloured 'sea parrots', otherwise known as puffins."

Mark Reid
April 2003

WALK INFORMATION

. . . .

Points of interest:	A trio of fishing villages, 18th Century lime-kilns, nature reserves, 'going for a kip', the sanctuary of St Cuthbert, puffin island, a daring sea rescue, the palace of the Kings of Northumbria, the birthplace of the RNLI and four magnificent golden strands.

Distance:

Embleton to Beadnell	5 miles
Beadnell to Bamburgh	6 miles
Total	11 miles

Time: Allow 5 - 6 hours

Terrain: This walks follows the coastal path all the way from Embleton to Bamburgh with several long stretches across wide beaches. Beach walking can be tiring, especially if the sand is soft, and care must be taken during bad weather or high tides.

Beach Access: The route has been described using Rights of Way, some of which run behind sand dunes or along the coastal road; these sections are therefore recommended as 'bad weather / high tide' alternatives. The best way to complete this walk is along the beaches - access points and directions along the beach have been given in italics within the route description (marked by *), thus allowing you to choose your route.

NB: Please see the note on Page 13 concerning Rights of Way, Access and Beaches. The sand dune ecology is fragile do not walk across them.

Tide Times:	See local newspapers or call the Coastguard 24-hr Information Line: 0870 6006 505
Ascents:	There are no significant ascents along this walk.
Viewpoints:	Embleton Bay looking back towards Dunstanburgh Castle. Newton Point looking back across Embleton Bay. The wide sweep of Beadnell Bay towards Beadnell Harbour. Sea views from the ruins of St Ebba's Chapel. The Farne Islands and Bamburgh Castle from the glorious stretch of beach between Seahouses and Bamburgh.

FACILITIES

· ·

Embleton	Inn / B&B / Shop / P.O. / Café / Bus / Phone / Toilets / Camp
Low Newton-by-the-Sea	Inn / Phone / Toilets
Beadnell	Inn / B&B / Shop / P.O. / Café / Bus / Phone / Toilets / Camp
Seahouses	Inn / B&B / Shop / P.O. / Café / Bus / Phone / Toilets / Info.
Bamburgh	Inn / B&B / Shop / P.O. / Café / Bus / Phone / Toilets / Camp

ROUTE DESCRIPTION

(Map Nine)

From Embleton, head back along the lane towards Embleton Bay and the beach, passing the Sportsman Hotel on your right, down to reach Dunstanburgh Castle Golf Club at the end of the lane *(Beach Route from this point *)*. Head through the gate out onto the golf course then turn immediately left (SP 'Low Newton-by-the-Sea') and follow the boundary / fence of the golf course as it gently curves round to the right then, where the fence turns sharp left (at the foot of the bank), turn left along a track climbing steadily up (still heading alongside the boundary of the golf course) then at the top of the bank follow the boundary of the golf course to the right then bending round to the left to reach a fence across your path overlooking Newton Pool Nature Reserve. Turn right along this path alongside the fence down passing a bird hide then on to join a track just after a cottage. Follow this track straight on, which soon becomes a lane that leads on passing a row of cottages on your right then turns to the right on to reach the main road at Low Newton-by-the-Sea (pub to your right in the 'square' of cottages).

Beach Route - Embleton to Low Newton: *After the gate at the end of the lane, head straight on across the golf course towards the beach then turn left immediately before the FB across Embleton Burn. Follow this clear path on with the stream on your right for a short distance then follow this wide stream (The Skaith) bending to the right through a break in the dunes onto the beach. Turn left along the beach and follow it all the way to reach the 'square' of cottages at Low Newton-by-the-Sea.*

Walk up along the main road heading away from the Square and beach then, after a short distance, take the FP to the right (SP 'Beadnell' / National Trust sign 'Newton Point') through a kissing gate. Follow the clear grassy path bearing up to the left, over a stile beside a gate after which continue on alongside the fence / wall on your left (Coastguard Lookout across to your left). Continue on alongside this wall and follow it as it drops down beneath some low crags to reach a stile beside a gate.

After the gate, head on along the clear grassy path to the left meandering through low dunes (keep to the clear path) then on alongside a stone wall on your left to reach the large parking area beside Newton Links House. Head across the car park, through a kissing gate and down onto a track. *(Beach Route from this point *)* Head straight on over this track through a kissing gate / stile ahead (National Trust sign 'Newton Links') and follow the wide clear grassy track straight on passing Newton Links House on your left on to soon reach another stile beside a gate. Head over the stile and continue straight on along the wide grassy track running behind the dunes on to reach a large FB across Long Nanny (stream) after about three quarters of a mile. After the FB, continue on along the clear grassy track bearing to the right (SP 'Beadnell') then straight on keeping close to the fence on your left, with the dunes across to your right, to reach a large caravan park. Follow the lane straight on through the caravan park (waymarkers) to eventually reach a road at the entrance to the park. Head straight on along the road, passing a parking area and toilets on your right, and follow this on bearing round to the left (passing the turning for Beadnell Harbour) to run along the coast (with the sea to your right) for approx. 0.5 miles to reach the road junction with the B1340 (Beadnell village short detour to the left just before this junction).

*Beach Route - Newton Links House to Beadnell: *Turn right along the track after the car park and follow this down onto the beach. Turn left along the top edge of the beach keeping close to the dunes. About 200 yards before the sand dunes begin to curve round into the broad fan of the Long Nanny (deep stream) which cuts across the beach, turn left up along a narrow path across the sand dunes (following the line of a temporary fence across the beach & dunes during the summer breeding season) that leads to a stile at a corner of a fence. (The banks and estuary of the Long Nanny are protected as a Nature Reserve - keep within this fence-line). Cross the stile and follow this fence line (with the fence on your right) to reach a large FB across the Long Nanny. After the FB, follow the clear grassy track bearing to the right (SP 'Beadnell') then straight on keeping close to the fence on your left for about 0.25 miles then, where another fence joins from the left beside two gates, turn sharp right along a clear narrow access path that leads across the dunes and through a* *bridlegate back onto the beach. Follow the broad sweeping bay round to join a road beside the disused limekilns at Beadnell Harbour. Turn left and follow this coastal road away from the Harbour then at the junction follow the coastal road to the right (with the sea on your right) for approx. 0.5 miles to reach a T-junction with the B1340 (Beadnell village short detour to the left just before this junction).*

(Map Ten)

At the T-junction with the B1340, turn right along the road *(Beach Route from this point *)* and follow this road straight on to reach Annstead Bridge (across Annstead Burn) after about a mile. Continue straight on along the road then take the FP to the right immediately after Seahouses Golf Club on your right (SP 'Seahouses Harbour'). Follow the clearly marked path across the Golf Course passing some small ponds on your left at first then on down to join the beach beside five Second World War concrete blocks (if foreshore impassable, return to the road and follow it into Seahouses). Turn left across the foreshore, keeping close to the low cliffs, for a short distance then follow the path up through a gap in the low cliffs (waymarker) back onto the golf course. Follow the clearly marked path straight on across the golf course to reach a small gate at the end of the golf course, then head on along the coastal path to reach Seahouses Harbour.

* Beach Route – Beadnell to Seahouses: *from the T-junction at the top end of Beadnell turn right along the B1340 then, after a short distance, a path leads off to the right down onto the beach. Turn left along the beach and follow it sweeping round then, as you approach the low cliffs at the northern end of the beach, ford the shallow waters of Annstead Burn to join a footpath just to the right of a row of five Second World War concrete blocks below the low cliffs (if Annstead Burn is impassable, a path leads up alongside the burn to Annstead Bridge –see above for route from this bridge). At the concrete blocks, turn right across the foreshore, keeping close to the low cliffs on your left, for a short distance then follow the path up through a gap in the low cliffs onto the golf course. Follow the clearly marked path straight on across the golf course to reach a small gate at the end of the golf course, then head on along the coastal path to reach Seahouses Harbour.*

Skirt around the Harbour and head up to reach the main road in the centre of Seahouses, then follow this road (B1340) northwards along the coast heading out of the town *(Beach Route from this point *)*. Carry straight on along this road heading northwards passing Monks House after just over a mile then continue on along the wide grassy verge beside the road all the way to Bamburgh.

** **Beach Route - Seahouses to Bamburgh:** Follow the main B1340 out of Seahouses then, just before you leave the houses behind, follow the footpath that bears away from the road to the right across the top of low cliffs then leads down to join the southern end of the beach. Follow this wide beach northwards passing Monks House after about a mile then on passing across Greenhill Rocks (backed by high sand dunes) and continue on along the broad beach to reach Bamburgh Castle. Follow the beach passing to the right of the Castle then head to the left skirting around the Castle along a wide path that leads through the dunes (lifebelt) on beneath the northern ramparts of the Castle to join a footpath which you follow to the left across the Cricket Ground into Bamburgh.*

Low Newton-by-the-Sea

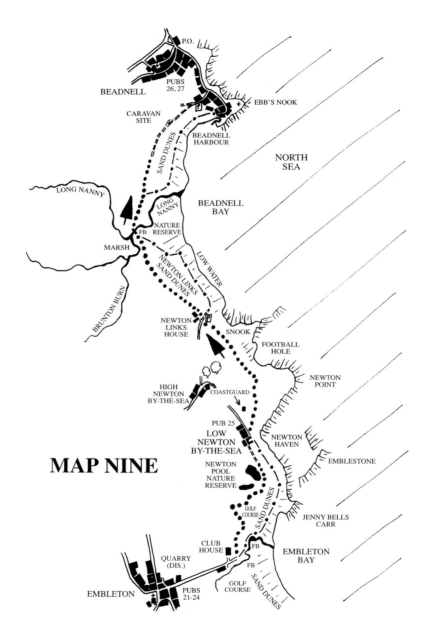

MAP NINE

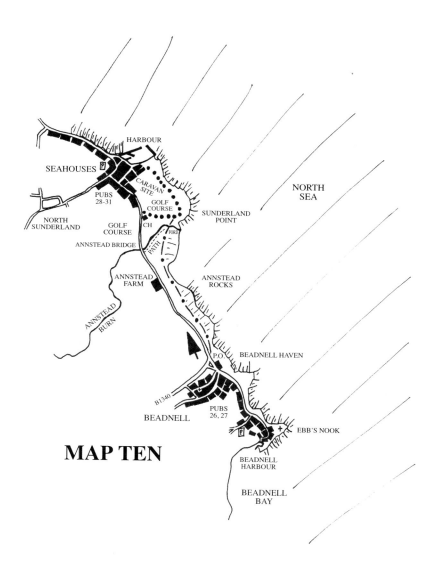

HARBOUR

SEAHOUSES

CARAVAN SITE

PUBS 28-31

NORTH SUNDERLAND

GOLF COURSE

GOLF COURSE

CH

FORD

PATH

ANNSTEAD BRIDGE

SUNDERLAND POINT

NORTH SEA

ANNSTEAD FARM

ANNSTEAD ROCKS

ANNSTEAD BURN

BEADNELL HAVEN

P.O.

B1340

BEADNELL

PUBS 26, 27

EBB'S NOOK

BEADNELL HARBOUR

MAP TEN

BEADNELL BAY

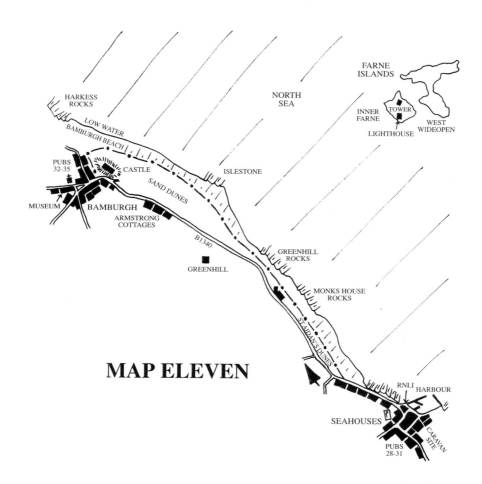

MAP ELEVEN

LOW NEWTON-BY-THE-SEA lies hidden away at the end of a narrow country lane, a delightful square of old fishermen's cottages looking out across the sheltered bay of Newton Haven with its fine sandy beach hemmed in by shelving fingers of rock. An old 19th Century coastguard lookout station sits atop the high ground overlooking the bay, from where there are wonderful views back towards Dunstanburgh Castle. This village is one of Northumberland's hidden gems with well-kept cottages facing across a small green and a wonderful old pub tucked away in the corner; but it has not always been like this. These cottages were originally built in the 18th Century for local farm workers who then supplemented their income by fishing for shellfish and herring from the Haven. During the 1840's, the cottages were 'improved' with the addition of an upper floor and dormer windows whilst the old yards to the side of each cottage, where fish were once gutted and lobster pots stored, were filled-in to create a continuous square. *"Newton is not pretty or pleasing: it boasts a coast-guard station, and exhibits itself to the sea as a village of pantiled cottages and stables, along three sides of a square, where only the public-house has an upper storey. A shabby shed occupies part of the open space, and all round it the women fling their household slops and fish offal; and having created an abomination, are content to live within sight thereof."* **(Walter White 'Northumberland and The Border' 1859).** Sadly, there are no fishermen living in the square today although some still use the Haven to catch crab and lobster. Just to the south-west of Low Newton is Newton Pool Nature Reserve, which has developed into an important breeding ground for birds, newts, frogs, dragonflies and rare plants since it was established as a reserve back in 1972. It is particularly noted for its migratory birds, many of which can be viewed in season from the bird hide. This Nature Reserve, along with much of the coastline and Low Newton village itself is owned and protected by The National Trust.

BEADNELL BAY is perhaps the finest beach along Northumberland's coastline, a wonderful dune-backed strand of golden sands curving gently round for over two miles from Snook Point to Beadnell Harbour; the sheer size of the beach means that it never gets crowded. *"At Beadnell Harbour, near the bungalows, perhaps half a dozen* *people were sitting on the beach. I walked on for several miles round the bay, over the firm white sands, without encountering a soul or seeing a single habitation. Accustomed as I am to the crowded beaches of Southern England, where every agreeable stretch of coast line is strewn with villas, and made accessible by omnibuses, this solitude was impressive.* **(Douglas Goldring 'A Tour in Northumbria' 1938).** The grassy track that runs behind the dunes once formed part of the main road to Alnwick via Beadnell and Low Newton before the Turnpike roads were built in the 18th Century. The Long Nanny cuts a wide and ever-changing channel through the dunes and across the beach, although a footbridge offers a way across this deep burn. The flat salt marshes, sand dune system and the broad fanning waters of the Long Nanny are now protected as a Nature Reserve by The National Trust due to its importance as a breeding site, especially during the spring and summer, for little terns, artic terns, ringed plover, reed bunting, stonechat, skylark and meadow pipit. The Reserve is becoming increasingly important during the winter months as a breeding site for snow bunting. The National Trust also protects the sand dune system to the south of the Long Nanny known as Newton Links, which is one of several narrow dune systems along this stretch of coastline. Coarse grasses such as Marram Grass and Lyme Grass trap the wind-blown sand, which then develops over time into a mound with the grass loosely binding the sand together to create a thin layer of lime-rich soil that also supports rare plants such as orchids. The dunes are very fragile and once damaged are quickly eroded.

BEADNELL HARBOUR has the distinction of being the only harbour along the entire East Coast that faces west, protected by the rocky arm of St Ebb's Nook. Local fishermen have used this sheltered bay for centuries, however, it was not until 1798 that a small harbour was built. In the same year, Richard Pringle was granted permission from John Wood, the local landowner, to build a large limekiln on the pier; this proved to be so successful that two more kilns were built. As farming improved during 18th Century, lime was needed to 'sweeten' the soils and so improve yields. Limestone was plentiful along the Northumberland coast, so the production of lime became big business during the late 18th and early 19th Centuries. To make lime, limestone and coal were burnt together to produce a lime ash, known as quicklime, which was then used in agriculture and as a building material. The limestone and coal were sourced from local quarries and then transported to the harbour via a tramway along what is now Harbour Road to be exported to other British ports along with local goods such as wood, grain, fish and shellfish. However, within a few decades the kilns had fallen into disuse, although the herring industry had begun to flourish and Beadnell soon became one of the busiest fishing villages along the coast with scores of fishermen and three herring yards set around the harbour. The distinctive house of Beach Court with its small tower stands on the site of an old herring yard. During the early 20th Century the herring industry began to slowly decline, although this was balanced by a growth in tourism. New houses were built along the coast road with little consideration for the architectural heritage of the old harbour area. Today, only a handful of cobles work out of the harbour fishing for salmon, lobster and crab; the old limekilns have found a new lease of life as stores for lobster pots and fishing gear. Perhaps Beadnell Harbour has lost some of its soul to tourism, as the large car park and vast caravan site testify, however, there is a place nearby that offers the opportunity for quiet contemplation with only the sound of rushing waves and seagulls for company. A path leads from beside the limekilns onto Ebb's Nook, a grassy promontory that has been a place of worship for centuries. A ruined 13th Century chapel lies buried beneath the grass, its outline still clearly visible along with sections of masonry. This is thought to the site of a 7th Century church associated with St Ebba, the Anglo-Saxon princess and sister of the Northumbrian kings Oswald and Oswy. It was Oswald who re-introduced Christianity to his kingdom of Northumbria and Ebba, like many aristocratic women of her time, chose to convert and become a nun. She went on to become the first Abbot of the monastery at Coldingham and was also a friend of St Cuthbert. There are many sites associated with Ebba throughout Northumberland.

BEADNELL VILLAGE lies just inland from the harbour, at the heart of which is St Ebb's Church, an imposing Georgian church with a distinctive pierced octagonal Gothic screen around the base of its tower.

Hidden behind the church is Church Cottages, a square of attractive houses overlooking the old village green. There has been a settlement here since pre-Conquest days probably centred around the Saxon chapel on St Ebb's Nook. Evidence for this early settlement is sketchy and it was not until medieval times that a village developed, indeed Beadnell is surrounded by medieval ridge and furrow ploughing strips and boasts the remains of three medieval buildings including St Ebb's Chapel on the headland as well as the Craster Arms and Beadnell Hall in the village itself, which both incorporate defensive towers. Beadnell Hall dates back to the 14th Century, although the present building is predominantly Georgian. This fine house with its striking gables was once the home of the Wood family who were succeeded by the Craster family as landowners. This hall was latterly used as a hotel but has recently been developed into apartments. Next door is the large Victorian Beadnell House, now a hotel, beyond which is the Craster Arms, a fine example of a medieval tower house that dates back to at least the 16th Century. Despite later modifications, it still retains its defensive stature with stout walls and the large crest of the Craster family high on its frontage. Beadnell enjoyed its greatest period of prosperity during the 18th and 19th Centuries when the limekilns were in full production, the herring industry flourished and smuggling was at its height! Smuggling was once big business here; in 1762 Excisemen seized 2,700 gallons of illegal brandy in a single night - it must have been quite a party! As the Harbour was small and away from the village, local fishermen from Beadnell launched their cobles from Beadnell Haven, a small sandy cove set within the rocky foreshore just to the east of the village (to the side of the Post Office along the coast road). There was once a square of fishermen's cottages here, however, they were demolished many years ago although several old wooden tarred sheds survive, which were used (and still are) for storing fishing equipment. *"The occupation of the villagers is well seen by the drawn-up cobles, the outspread nets, the lobster-pots lying about in heaps, the sheds, constructed of old fishing-boats as receptacles for the yarns and lines and other fishing-gear, and the big cauldrons, with stumpy chimneys, for heating the tar."* **(William Weaver Tomlinson 'Comprehensive Guide to**

Northumberland' 1888). To the north of Beadnell a curving bay sweeps up towards North Sunderland Point backed by Annstead Dunes, an important sand dune system with dunes up to 30-ft high in places that are now protected by the Northumberland Wildlife Trust.

Beadnell Harbour

SEAHOUSES is a bustling harbour and seaside resort, famed for its kippers, fish and chips, fine sandy beaches and boat trips to the Farne Islands. But look beyond the amusement arcades and you will discover a fishing village steeped in history. Following the Norman Conquest, the Saxon fortress of Bamburgh became a Royal castle surrounded by large estates. A small village soon developed at the southern end of these estates and became known as Sunderland or 'southern lands', later given the prefix 'North'. For several centuries it remained a small farming community with many of the farmers supplementing their income by inshore fishing in the sheltered haven just to the east of the village, where the present harbour now stands. This natural harbour was, and still is, called North Sunderland Seahouses. One of the oldest buildings in Seahouses is the Olde Ship Hotel, built in 1745 as a farmhouse overlooking the harbour, gaining its drinks licence in 1812. It is an absolute gem of a pub, packed full of nautical memorabilia including the name-board of the Forfarshire. In 1768 a lease was acquired to take coal and limestone from quarries to the south of the village and build a group of limekilns beside the harbour area, which soon became busy exporting lime. In the late 18th Century a stone pier was built, replacing an earlier wooden jetty, to provide a larger harbour for the flourishing lime trade. Within a hundred years the limekilns had closed down; they are now used by local fishermen to store their lobster pots and nets. *"Lime is the principal article of trade; and the kilns are built close to the harbour for convenience of loading, and for the inconvenience of the town, which gets well smothered with the smoke whenever the wind blows from the sea."* **(Walter White 1859).** By the 1880's, Seahouses had become such a busy fishing port, particularly for herring, that the Crewe Trustees (see Bamburgh Castle) gave money to improve the Harbour with the construction of a breakwater and large outer pier complete with a small lighthouse, which enclosed the original 18th Century piers to create an Inner and Outer Harbour. At its height in the 1890's, some 300 herring cobles were using the harbour, which would have been bursting at the seams with fishing boats, fishermen and barrels of salted herring on the quayside waiting to be loaded onto boats - over 6,000 barrels of herring were shipped out in one year! There were a dozen or so herring yards and smokehouses clustered around the maze of streets immediately to the south of the harbour around Crewe Street, Union Street and South Street. Just imagine the mess and smell! *"At Seahouses is an extensive fish-curing establishment, a fact which proclaims itself unmistakably as you near the village, especially if the day chance to be at all warm."* **(Jean F. Terry, 'Northumberland, Yesterday and To-day', 1913).** These old streets have changed little in the intervening years with unmade roads and small squares of early 19th Century fishermen's cottages including the delightful Craster Square along South Street. Just up from here is the last remaining smokehouse in Seahouses where you can buy the famous Swallow's kippers made in the traditional way in an original 19th Century smokehouse by this long-established family business. According to local folklore, the first kipper was produced at Seahouses when some herrings were accidentally left in a shed overnight where there was a smouldering fire. In the 1890's the North Sunderland Railway opened, a private railway formed by a group of local fishermen and merchants who decided to 'go it alone' after failing to persuade the North Eastern Railway to build a branch line to Seahouses. They built a four-mile railway from the East Coast line at Chathill to Seahouses Station (which was situated where the large car park now is across the road from the harbour) to open up new markets for fish and help exploit the newly extended harbour. The railway prospered between the wars exporting fish from the harbour and bringing tourists to the village, attracted by the glorious beaches and nearby Farne Islands. Initially, fishermen and their families would take visitors in to help supplement their income, then larger hotels and boarding houses were built around the old fishing village. *"It is now high summer, but an autumn day comes back to me on this same shore road when the fern-clad dunes were aflame with gold, and the sea lay behind them with glassy surface unstirred by the faintest breath of air. And close to the shore the whole of the Scottish herring-fleet lay hopelessly becalmed on their southern journey – some forty or fifty vessels floating motionless and at all angles within biscuit-throw of one another."* **(A. G. Bradley, 'The Romance of Northumberland', 1908).** In the years following the Second World War the local herring industry had all but collapsed due to declining stocks coupled with competition from larger trawlers; as the fishing industry waned so did the fortunes of the railway and it finally closed in 1951. The harbour area is a fascinating place to wander through with its stacks of lobster pots, fishing nets and brightly-painted booths offering trips to the Farne Islands. It is still a working fishing port, although many of the old fishing boats have found a new lease of life taking visitors out to the Farne Islands. Just above the harbour is the RNLI Lifeboat Station where you can see the Mersey Class 'Grace Darling'. This Lifeboat Station was established in 1827 by the Crewe Trustees and given to the RNLI in 1852, since when it has saved the lives of hundreds of people in the treacherous seas around this rocky coastline.

THE FARNE ISLANDS lie scattered off the coast, a collection of twenty-eight small islands, although this shrinks to fifteen at high tide! Most of the islands are little more than jagged outcrops of hard rock, the last flurry of the Great Whin Sill, although one or two have a covering of grass. There are two main groups of islands, the Inner Farnes consisting of West and East Wideopen, Scarcar and Inner Farne whilst two miles further out are the Outer Farnes, consisting of Staple Island, Brownsman, North and South Wamses, Big Harcar and Longstone. The Farne Islands have three claims to fame: saints, heroines and birds! St Aidan, the first Bishop of Lindisfarne, visited Inner Farne during the 7th Century to find spiritual solitude then later in the same century St Cuthbert built a small hermit's cell, guest house and landing place for boats on the island. St Cuthbert died on Inner Farne in 687 and was buried at Lindisfarne Priory, his body later moved to escape Vikings raids before a final resting place was found at Durham. In 1246 a small Benedictine monastery was established on Inner Farne, a daughter house of Durham, which existed until the Dissolution of the Monasteries in 1536, after which it was granted to the Dean and Chapter of Durham Cathedral who owned them until 1861 when they were sold to Charles Thorp, Archdeacon of Durham. The islands were acquired by The National Trust in 1925 and are now protected as a Nature Reserve. This tradition dates back to St Cuthbert who loved and protected the many sea birds and seals on the islands, indeed, eider ducks are still locally known as Cuddy ducks. In less enlightened times, eggs were stolen during the breeding season, however, Archdeacon Thorp employed wardens to protect the birds, since when the islands have become an internationally important bird sanctuary. An amazing 274 species of birds have been recorded here including fulmars, guillemots, razorbills, cormorants, kittiwakes, shags, eiders, gulls, terns, auks, ringed plovers, oystercatchers, puffins and rock pipits. During the spring and summer nesting season, the islands are home to over twenty different species of breeding sea birds as well as a staggering seventy thousand puffins! During the early winter months the islands also support an important breeding colony of grey seals. It is a memorable experience to bob around the islands in an old fishing boat to get a 'bird's eye view' of the squawking colonies of nesting birds as well as seals basking on the rocks. The largest island is Inner Farne with its lighthouse, tower house and monastic remains where visitors can disembark to get an even closer look at the birds. *"Few people, one would imagine, would care to pass by the Farne Islands, which lie off the coast north-east of North Sunderland and Bamborough, especially as there is a spice of danger attaching to an expedition to them in the fact that if rough weather should happen to spring up after visitors are landed on them, a stay of some days under the most primitive conditions may be necessitated."* **(J. S. Fletcher 'The Enchanting North' 1908).** There are the remains of four medieval buildings on Inner Farne including St Cuthbert's Chapel, St Mary's Chapel, Prior Castell's Tower and a guest house. The first 'official' lighthouse on the islands was a beacon on Prior Castell's Tower in 1673, although it is said that hermits on the islands would light beacons during bad weather as far back as the 9th Century. The lighthouse later moved to Staple Island, then onto Brownsman in 1783 and finally onto Longstone in 1826; the Farne Islands today boast two automatic lighthouses with the white-washed Inner Farne lighthouse (1809) and the red and white Longstone Lighthouse (1826). The Farne Islands will always be associated with Grace Darling, one of this country's most famous heroines. Grace was born in 1815 at Bamburgh, shortly after which her family moved to the desolate Brownsman Island, where her father William was the lighthouse keeper, then again in 1826 the family moved to the new lighthouse on Longstone. At 4am on the 7th of September 1838 the steam ship Forfarshire, sailing up the coast with passengers and cargo, struck the Big Harcar rock during a violent storm. In the early morning light, Grace looked out from the lighthouse and saw the wreck and several survivors clinging to the rock. Her father thought the conditions were too bad for the North Sunderland Lifeboat to be launched and so decided that he and Grace had to go to their rescue. They launched their small coble into the treacherous seas battling against strong winds to reach the wreck, heroically rescuing nine people who were brought back to the lighthouse. Newspapers reported the daring rescue, often embellished with exaggerated claims, and she soon became a national heroine with people visiting the Farne Islands to catch a glimpse of her. Sadly, on the 20th of October 1842 she died of Consumption at the young age of 26 and lies buried in the churchyard at Bamburgh.

BAMBURGH BEACH sweeps northwards from Seahouses to beyond Bamburgh, with Bamburgh Castle dominating the scene. This is an exhilarating walk with crashing waves, miles of golden sand, high dunes, the Farne Islands just out to sea and Holy Island on the horizon.

The highlight is the approach to Bamburgh Castle with its towering ramparts perched on a huge outcrop of rock. The beach is backed by an extremely high range of sand dunes known as St Aidan's Dunes, with the old farmhouse of Monks House sheltering in a gap between the dunes. In 1257 land was granted to the monks of Inner Farne by Henry III where they established a small grange, or monastic farmhouse, and also operated a ferry out to the Farne Islands. The present buildings date mainly from the 19th Century, during which time the farmhouse was also used as a hostelry known as St Cuthbert's Inn.

Bamburgh Castle

BAMBURGH is dominated by Bamburgh Castle, an awe-inspiring fortress of soaring ramparts and towers perched magnificently on a dramatic outcrop of the Great Whin Sill right on the coast; it is little wonder that this strategic defensive outcrop has been utilised for over two millennia. *"Bamburgh Castle, as a mere spectacle, has no rival in Britain; and in the significance of ancient story, scarcely any. It combines the vastness of Alnwick or Caerphilly with the pose of Harlech or Cerrig Cennen. For its stands in sublime isolation on a huge whinstone crag some one hundred and fifty feet above the waves which break at its feet, while on the landward side the cliff is so precipitous that a coin dropped from some of the castle windows would fall directly upon the green far below."* **(A. G. Bradley 1908)**. At first glance it appears to be a complete medieval castle, however, paradoxically it is both less and more historical than it looks!

The magnificent Keep is all that remains of the original stone Norman castle, its four-metre thick walls withstood the cannon fire that destroyed much of the castle during the War of the Roses, indeed, much of what we see today is the result of rebuilding work carried out during the 18th and 19th Centuries. This outcrop of Whin Sill has been used as a defensive site since pre-Roman times when it was known as Din Guardi, the stronghold of a local Iron Age Celtic chieftain. All of this was to change with the arrival of the Saxons and Angles from across the North Sea during the 6th Century; there are romantic stories that link King Arthur with this fortress during these turbulent times between the native British and invading English. In 547 the Saxon chieftain King Ida 'the Flamebearer' landed his ships on the North East coast, quickly conquered the ancient Celtic kingdoms of Northern Britain and took control of Din Guardi where he built his wooden fortress, establishing a new Saxon kingdom of Bernicia. Ida's grandson King Ethelfrith gave this fortress to his wife, Queen Bebba, after whom it was named - Bebba's Burgh. By the end of Ethelfrith's reign in the early 7th Century they had also taken control of the kingdom of Deira to the south of Bernicia, thus creating a Saxon kingdom that stretched from the River Humber northwards to the Firth of Forth, and they called it 'Northumbria'. Bamburgh was the capital of this kingdom, and it was here that the ancient kings were crowned. The kingdom of Northumbria retained its two regions of Bernicia and Deira, which both had their own Royal families who, despite being related, were often at war! When Oswald, son of Ethelfrith, became King of Northumbria in 634 he united Bernicia and Deira as one Christian kingdom and invited the monks of Iona to send a missionary to convert his people. St Aidan came and established a monastery on Lindisfarne as well as a church at Bamburgh. Thus followed the 'Golden Age of Northumbria' when this region became a centre of great learning and culture. During the 9th and 10th Centuries, frequent Vikings raids along the coast brought this 'Golden Age' crashing to an end; they ransacked the monasteries and took control of Deira, the southern half of Northumbria, which they then ruled from Jorvik (York), although Bernicia continued to be ruled from Bamburgh until 1076. In the late 11th Century, William II marched northwards, seized Northumberland and ordered a formidable stone castle to be constructed as a defence against the Scots to replace the old wooden Saxon fortress, although it was captured by the Scots on a number of occasions. By the reign of Henry II in the late 12th Century, this Norman castle was firmly in English control and had developed into a mighty fortress with a curtain wall stretching a full quarter of a mile across the outcrop enclosing a huge square Keep, Great Hall and Chapel plus many other buildings. Throughout the turbulent medieval period, especially at the height of the Border Troubles, this impregnable Royal castle played an important role with many kings of England staying here. During the War of the Roses the castle remained loyal to Henry VI, however, the Lancastrian forces surrendered to Edward IV's army in 1464 after a bombardment; it was the first castle in England to fall to artillery fire. The castle remained Crown property, due to its strategic position, until the Union of the Crowns in 1603, after which it was given to Claudius Forster, Warden of the Middle Marches whose grandfather had been appointed Governor of the Castle by Elizabeth I for services to the Crown. Sadly, the Forster family allowed the castle to fall into ruin mainly because of their extravagant lifestyle which forced them into financial difficulties. When they were declared bankrupt in 1704, Lord Crewe, Prince Bishop of Durham who was married to Dorothy Forster, bought the castle. The Forster family became famous when Tom Forster, an inexperienced soldier who had been made a General due to his influential family name, led the Northumbrian rebels during the 1715 Jacobite Uprising. He was soon captured and taken prisoner to Newgate Gaol by the King's forces. His sister, also called Dorothy and the niece of Lord Crewe and Dorothy Forster, famously rescued him from prison by dressing him as her maid when she went to visit him! When Lord Crewe died in 1722 he left his wealth to the Crewe Trustees who were entrusted with the upkeep of the castle. Under the guidance of Dr John Sharp, Archdeacon of Northumberland, restoration of the castle began in the 1750's along with many other philanthropic deeds including a free school, infirmary, library, dispensary, windmill and coastguard station; in 1786 the world's first lifeboat station was established at Bamburgh out of Crewe Trust

Funds. In 1894 the castle was sold once again to Lord Armstrong, the great Victorian industrialist and inventor, who embarked on an ambitious restoration project including the rebuilding of the curtain walls, the State Rooms and the Great Hall. A tour of the castle is a 'must' to see the magnificent Victorian Great Hall with its collection of armour, Norman Keep, Crewe Museum Room and the Armstrong Museum. Of particular note is the Saxon well beneath the Keep, which is an amazing 145-ft deep excavated through solid whinstone rock that also doubled as an escape route in times of siege - not bad considering it was built 1,500 years ago! Bamburgh Castle is still the home of the Armstrong family.

St Aidan's Church stands on the western edge of Bamburgh, a place of worship and pilgrimage since the first wooden church was built on the site in 635AD when St Aidan was invited by King Oswald to bring Christianity to Northumbria. In 651AD Aidan fell ill and a shelter was built against the western gable of the wooden church where he died resting against a wooden beam. This beam then gained miraculous properties and is said to be incorporated into the present roof of the church above the font. After the Norman Conquest the church was rebuilt in stone and given to the Augustinian monks of Nostell Priory, Yorkshire in about 1121 - the kings of England believed it to be important to have control of this troubled Border region and so were keen to see a wealthy monastic order controlling the land. The small Norman church was replaced by a larger church in the late 12th and early 13th Centuries, essentially the church we see today. After the Dissolution of the Monasteries, all the church lands were sold to the Forster family and the church became the Parish Church. It is a beautiful building with striking Early English pointed arches in the spacious nave as well as a wealth of interesting features including a simple memorial at the spot where St Aidan died, whilst in the churchyard is the very ornate Gothic tomb of Grace Darling surrounded by iron railings. Opposite the church is the RNLI Grace Darling Museum. Opened in 1938 on the centenary of the rescue, this fascinating museum boasts a wealth of artefacts, historical records, personal items and memorabilia including the original coble used by

Grace and her father during the rescue. Just up from this museum is Horsley Cottage where Grace Horsley Darling was born in 1815, whilst overlooking the green near the red 'phone box is the cottage where she died. Next to the Church is Bamburgh Hall, a fine Georgian house that stands on the site of the medieval manorial hall where the Augustinian monks once held their courts. The village of Bamburgh lies on a gentle slope between the church and the towering castle, with attractive cottages and old inns looking out across a delightful triangular tree-shaded green known as The Grove. At the top of this green is a superb walled garden, which was once the gardens of the castle (note the datestone of 1693 above the doorway) and are still used as a garden centre, whilst at the bottom of the village is a cricket pitch right beneath the crags and ramparts of the castle. On the outskirts of the village along the Seahouses road is a small development of wooden boarded houses known as Armstrong Cottages that were built by Lord Armstrong for workers restoring the castle.

Seahouses

STAGE FOUR

BAMBURGH
to
WOOLER

✦

"After the long walk from Rothbury to the mouth of the Coquet, followed by the sweeping strands of the coastline punctuated by mighty castles and small fishing villages, I turned westwards into the heart of Northumberland. A gradual climb up alongside Waren Burn through tiny villages took me up onto the broad heights of Chatton Moor amongst the Black Lands of the central sandstone hills. Beyond the ruins of Brownridge Farm I crossed the brow of the ridge and there they were at last; I felt as though I had deserved this view. Rising and falling against the western sky, the domed grassy hills of the Cheviots stood silently across the horizon. Brooding, wild yet appealing, the anticipation of the following day welled up inside – a full day through these untamed border hills beckoned, and I could not wait. But, closer to hand and in finer detail was the beautiful valley of the River Till with Chatton reposing in the valley bottom, where the warmth of the fireside at the Percy Arms waited."

Mark Reid
November 2003

WALK INFORMATION

Points of interest:
The legend of the Laidley Worm, hidden wooded burns, the Great North Road, an ornithological house, the Black Lands of Chatton Moor and the first sight of the Cheviots, a lovely Estate village, the river with two names, defensive towers, mysterious rock art, glorious views from Weetwood Moor, bloody battles and royal palaces.

Distance:

Bamburgh to Lucker	4.5 miles
Lucker to Chatton	7 miles
Chatton to Wooler	4.5 miles
Total	16 miles

Time:
Allow 7 hours

Terrain:
From Bamburgh, this walk follow field paths and quiet country lanes all the way to Warenford, with some short sections through woodland. From Warenford, the route heads west through forest (small ford to cross) out onto the open moorland of Chatton Moor to reach the ruined farmhouse of Brownridge, from where old green lanes and tracks lead down to reach Chatton. Field paths then lead across the Till Valley (boggy in places) to Fowberry Tower where a quiet lane is followed up to the edge of Weetwood Moor. Clearly marked paths lead over the moor to Wooler. Both the East Coast Mainline and the A1 are crossed beneath bridges.

Ascents:

Chatton Moor:	170 metres
Weetwood Moor:	155 metres

134

Viewpoints:	Views back towards Bamburgh and across Budle Bay from Galliheugh Bank.
	Views across the Till Valley from Chatton Moor with the Cheviot Hills in the distance.
	Wonderful views of the Cheviot Hills from Weetwood Moor.

FACILITIES

· ·

Bamburgh	Inn / B&B / Shop / P.O. / Café / Bus / Phone / Toilets / Camp
Lucker	Inn / Phone
Warenford	Inn / Bus / Phone
Chatton	Inn / B&B / Shop / P.O. / Bus / Phone
Wooler	Inn / B&B / Shop / P.O. / Café / Bus / Phone / Toilets / Info / YH / Camp

Fowberry Tower

ROUTE DESCRIPTION

. . . .

(Map Twelve)

From the 'green' in the centre of Bamburgh, walk along Radcliffe Road passing the Church on your right and follow this road out of the village. Continue along this road (wide verge) for about 0.75 miles then, where the road bends to the right, turn left along a lane (SP 'Dukesfield') then after a short distance turn right over a stile across the hedge (SP 'Spindlestone Heughs'). Head straight on passing to the left of the rocky / wooded hill alongside a tumbledown wall on your right then drop down to a stile over a fence (just below some outcrops). After the stile, continue straight on bearing slightly to the right heading along the edge of the field / overgrown hedge on to reach another stile, after which head straight on (now with the hedge on your left) to reach a road. Turn left along the road then almost immediately right towards 'Waren Caravan Park' then, at the entrance to the caravan park, follow the road sharp left. Continue on along the road for about 200 yards then, where the caravan park ends on your right, head to the right through a bridle-gate (SP 'Spindlestone Mill'). Head straight on keeping close to the fence / hedge on your left heading through the caravan park down to reach a stile to your left over a fence at the end of the caravan park (do not follow the driveway up to the right). Cross the stile and turn immediately right heading down with the wall / woodland on your right through a gate then down through woodland with the outcrops of Spindlestone Heughs to your right down through a gate at the end of the woods, after which head straight on across the field to quickly reach another gate. After this gate, head on alongside a fence / woodland on your right to quickly reach a stile, after which head on along the field-edge (with woodland on your right) then after a short distance the path heads on into woodland bearing very slightly to the right then drops down to reach the road through a bridle-gate (SP). Turn left along the road to reach a junction opposite Spindlestone Mill, where you turn left and follow the road climbing up then bending to the right on to reach the hamlet of Spindlestone. As you reach the houses (where the road bends to the left into the hamlet) head to the right through a gap in the stone wall passing immediately to the right of the long stone-built garage (SP 'Bradford, Lucker'). Head straight on along the field edge alongside the buildings / wall on your left along a wide grassy track, through a gate then on across the next field alongside the hedge on your left to reach a bridle-gate that leads into woodland. Follow the path down bearing slightly to the left to reach a FB over a side-stream (Waren Burn across to your right) then head up to another bridle-gate at the end of the woods. Head straight on alongside the fence / woodland on your right then, as you approach the large barns and houses of Bradford, bear away from the field-edge to pass to the left of the large barn, immediately after which head to the right to join a gravel track that leads through a bridle-gate then on passing between the two stone cottages onto the road (SP 'Lucker'). Cross the road and head through the bridle-gate to the left just off the driveway directly opposite, after which turn right along the wide grassy path (passing the house on your right) alongside the fence / hedge on your right across two large fields to reach the road. At the road take the footpath opposite to the right over a stile (SP), then bear to the right across the field over a wide FB across the side-stream of Winlaw Burn then continue straight on, keeping close to Waren Burn on your right, to reach the railway bridge (East Coast Mainline) across Waren Burn. Follow the path beneath the bridge (metal walkway), after which head straight on through woodland keeping close to the stream to reach a stile that leads out onto a field. Head up the field alongside the fence / wooded stream on your right then, as you approach the houses, keep to the fence-line on your right heading down a low wooded bank to reach a stile across your path (house just to your left). Cross the stile then head straight on through woodland to quickly reach another stile that leads onto the road opposite the Apple Inn in the centre of Lucker.

(Map Thirteen)

_____

Turn left along the road passing the Apple Inn and out of the village then, just after the last house on your right (Lucker Mill), head to the right over a wall stile (halfway along the wall - SP 'Warenford') then head diagonally to the left across the field to a bridle-gate in the far corner. After this gate, head to the right along the field-edge with the wooded banks of Waren Burn on your right then, at the end of this field, continue straight on along a clear path through trees / undergrowth (river on your right). After about 0.25 miles the path emerges from this woodland back onto the field-edge where you continue on along the field-edge with the woodland on your right then, as you approach a fence (and bridle-gate) across your path, bear to the right down through the trees / undergrowth (keeping close to the fence on your left) to reach a bridle-gate through this fence in the bottom corner of the field (just above Waren Burn). Head through this gate then continue straight on along the field-edge (with woodland / Waren Burn still on your right) then, where these trees end on your right, turn right through a gate in the hedge. Head on with the fence / woodland on your right along the field-edge on to reach a grassy track across your path. Turn right over a FB across Waren Burn, immediately after which head left through a gate then head on bearing slightly to the right across the field to join the road through a gate opposite the houses on the outskirts of Warenford. Turn left along the road to quickly reach a T-junction in the centre of Warenford. At the T-junction, head straight on through the gates directly opposite (SP 'Twizell') along the driveway (old gatehouse on your right), then on into woodland passing beneath the A1 bridge (Waren Burn on your left), after which follow the drive bearing up to the right, with open fields on your right. As you approach Twizell House, where the metal fence on your right ends ('ha-ha' to your right), head to the left (SP) along a wide grassy path. Follow this clearly marked path through the trees then, where the path divides, follow the grassy path to the right up passing the house (and a small stone building) on your right to reach a clear track just beyond the house (waymarker). Turn left along this track then, where it forks, follow the right-hand track up then straight on at the next 'junction' of tracks up passing to the right of Twizell Farm to reach the road. Turn left along the road and follow it on passing some cottages after which the road becomes a rough lane that leads down to a ford / FB across Cocklaw Burn (SP 'Warenford, Brownridge').

Cross the FB beside the ford and follow the clear track climbing up to the left and round to the right then levelling out - continue straight on along this track then follow it bending round to the right to reach Quarry Plantation. Continue along the clear track over a small ford and into the forest then follow the track gradually bending round to the left then, as you approach a gate at the end of the forest, bear off the track to the left (waymarker) heading straight on through the trees to quickly reach a stile over a fence that leads out of the forest opposite the large barn. Head to the left of the barn and over a stile, after which head on across the open field, bearing very slightly to the right, on to reach a stile just to the right of a gate in the fence across your path (heading towards the large plantation on the hillside ahead of you). Cross the stile then over a small burn, after which head on to join the fence-line on your right which you follow up to reach a gate. Head straight on along the grassy track to reach the bottom left corner of Brownridge Plantation then continue on alongside the plantation on your right then skirt to the left of the ruinous Brownridge Farm to reach a gate just to the left of the buildings. Head through the gate then turn right through another gate in a fence (forest just across to your right), after which follow the rough grassy track ahead bearing to the left gradually dropping down across the moorland then, where the ground levels out (with a stone sheepfold ahead of you and Ramsey Crag across to your left), turn left alongside a fence-line on your right (waymarker). Follow the grassy path passing beneath the outcrops of Ramsey Crag then where this fence ends continue straight on along a rough path then, after a short distance, follow a sunken track down to the right to quickly reach a bridle-gate that leads over Coalhouses Burn. After the burn, bear right and head straight on alongside the fence / wall on your right, passing the ruinous foundations of Coalhouses to reach a gate. Head through the gate and follow the clear grassy track straight on down through a series of gates to reach a 'junction' of clear tracks just above Shielhope House.

At the 'junction' of clear tracks, turn right through the gate (waymarkers) then immediately left through another gate and follow the grassy track (Unclassified County Road) down passing Shielhope House on your right to join a clearer stony track after a gate. *(A short alternative route to avoid the gardens of Shielhope House - at the 'junction' of tracks head straight on along the clear track for 200 yards (passing Shielhope House) then turn right through the double gates onto the clear stony track; this short section is not a Right of Way but (at the time of writing) offers an alternative route around the house).* Follow this stony track down for just over a mile to reach the main road. Turn left over Chatton Bridge across the River Till up into Chatton. Walk up into the village passing the small 'green' on your left just after which (pub on the corner) turn right (SP 'Lowick, Berwick') heading out of the village then where the road bends to the right after a short distance take the track to the left (SP). Follow the grassy enclosed track straight on up to reach a gate, after which carry straight on along the grassy track alongside the fence on your right (open field to your left), through a bridle-gate then on to reach another gate across your path (SP 'Fowberry Tower'). Head through this gate and continue straight on, with a fence now on your left, through another gate then halfway across the next field turn left through a gate (where the fence ends and the hedge begins - waymarker). Head down the field alongside the fence on your left through a gate at the bottom of the field, after which bear to the right across boggy ground to reach the large levee beside the River Till. Head on with the river on your right, over a ladder stile and up onto the levee then walk straight on along the levee (with the river on your right) to reach a gate across your path and out onto a field. Head diagonally to the left across the field to reach a gate in the far left corner (beside the river) that leads onto a track. Turn right along the track with the river on your right, passing beneath Fowberry Bridge immediately after which head left up onto the road.

At the road, turn right (away from the bridge) and follow this road straight on for 1 mile down and up a large dip to reach a T-junction. Turn left along the road towards 'Belford' then, after about 400 yards, turn right through a gate (SP 'Weetwood Bank'). Follow the grassy track straight on up across the field through a gate in the wall then continue straight on passing to the left of a small plantation heading up over the gently rising hill of Weetwood Moor. Where the plantation ends continue straight on alongside the fence / tumbledown wall on your right passing another smaller plantation to reach a gate (Cheviot Hills come into view). Continue straight on along the clear grassy path ('St Cuthbert's Way' waymarkers) across moorland then, as you reach the brow of Weetwood Bank the path divides - continue straight on along a clear sunken path (waymarker) slanting down the hillside, through a bridle-gate then down to join a road on a sharp bend. Turn right down along the road to reach the main road (A697) on the outskirts of Wooler, where you head to the right over the road-bridge across Wooler Water then left up along The Peth into the town centre.

Warenford

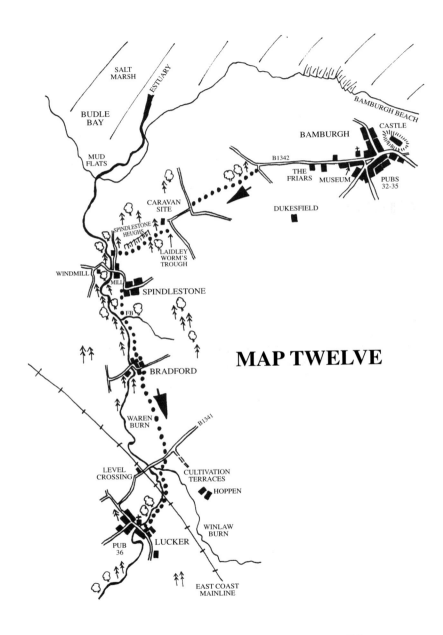

MAP TWELVE

SALT MARSH

ESTUARY

BUDLE BAY

MUD FLATS

BAMBURGH BEACH

CASTLE

BAMBURGH

B1342

THE FRIARS

MUSEUM

PUBS 32-35

DUKESFIELD

CARAVAN SITE

SPINDLESTONE HEUGHS

LAIDLEY WORM'S TROUGH

WINDMILL

MILL

SPINDLESTONE

FB

BRADFORD

WAREN BURN

B1341

LEVEL CROSSING

CULTIVATION TERRACES

HOPPEN

WINLAW BURN

PUB 36

LUCKER

EAST COAST MAINLINE

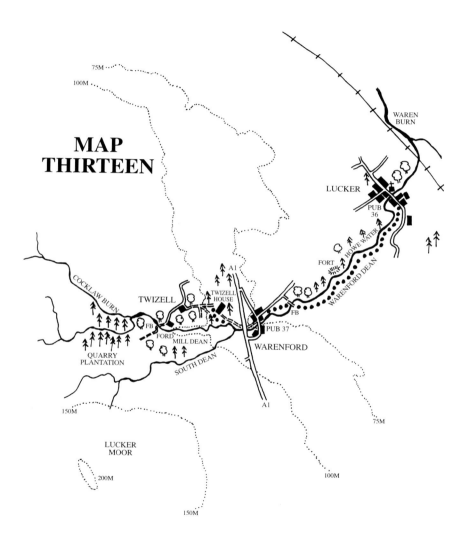

MAP
THIRTEEN

WAREN BURN

LUCKER

PUB 36

FORT

HOWE WATER

WARENFORD DEAN

COCKLAW BURN

TWIZELL

TWIZELL HOUSE

A1

FB

FB

FORD

MILL DEAN

PUB 37

WARENFORD

QUARRY PLANTATION

SOUTH DEAN

A1

75M
100M

150M

LUCKER MOOR

200M

150M

75M

100M

MAP
FOURTEEN

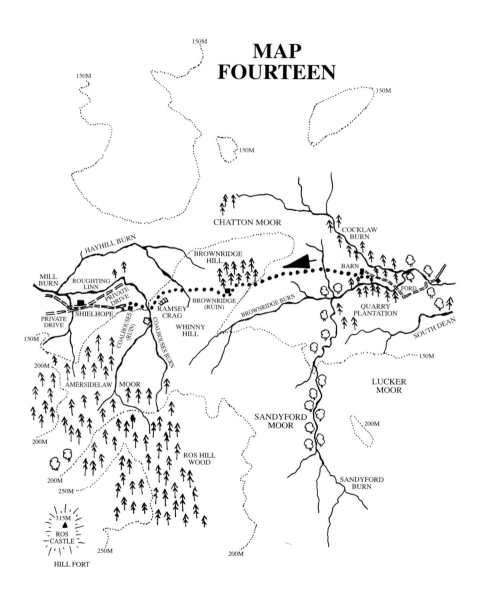

144

MAP
FIFTEEN

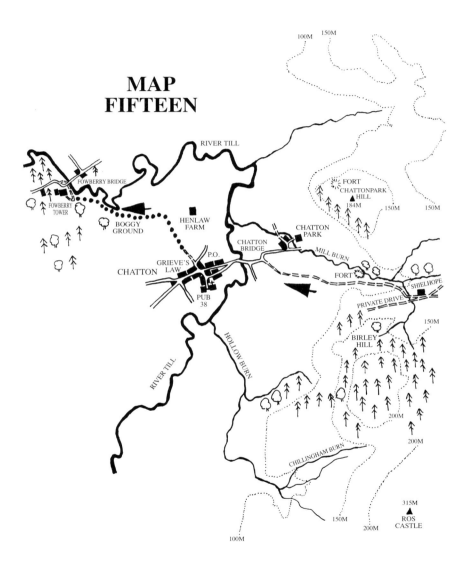

145

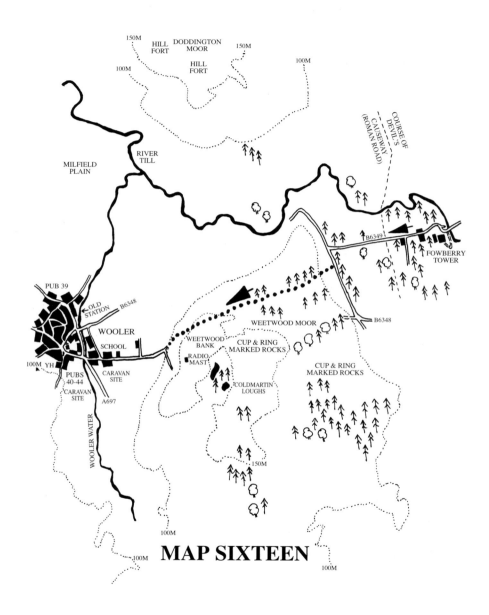

150M
HILL DODDINGTON
FORT MOOR
150M
HILL
FORT
100M
100M

COURSE OF
DEVIL'S
CAUSEWAY
(ROMAN ROAD)

RIVER
TILL

MILFIELD
PLAIN

B6349
FOWBERRY
TOWER

PUB 39

OLD
STATION
B6348

WOOLER

SCHOOL

WEETWOOD MOOR

B6348

100M YH

WEETWOOD
BANK

CUP & RING
MARKED ROCKS

CUP & RING
MARKED ROCKS

RADIO
MAST

PUBS
40-44

CARAVAN
SITE

COLDMARTIN
LOUGHS

CARAVAN
SITE

A697

WOOLER WATER

150M

100M

100M

MAP SIXTEEN

100M

SPINDLESTONE HEUGHS lies just to the south of Budle Bay, an outcrop of cliffs and crags formed by the Great Whin Sill, beneath which runs a wooded ravine down towards Waren Burn. This was the scene of one of Northumberland's most famous stories, the legend of the 'Laidley Worm'. *"An ancient ballad, composed by one Duncan Fraser, living on the Cheviot in the days of Bruce, seems to be the authority for the tale, and in a more modern shape it jingles quaintly through fifty verses embalmed in Northumbrian lore."* **(A. G. Bradley 'The Romance of Northumberland' 1908).** Many centuries ago, the King of Bamburgh, a widower with a beautiful daughter, married an attractive and sympathetic woman who turned out to be an evil witch! Jealous of the beauty of Princess Margaret, her new stepdaughter, she turned her into a "laidley worm" (or a 'loathsome serpent'). This serpent terrorised the district, devastating villages wherever it went as it searched for food, returning every night to its cave amongst the crags of Spindlestone Heughs. To stop the worm destroying their crops, locals filled a huge trough below the crags each evening with the milk from seven cows. News of this terrible beast spread far and wide and the Princess' brother, the Childe Wynde, who was abroad seeking his fortune, heard the news and set sail for home. His boat had masts made from rowan trees, which prevented the evil spells of the wicked witch from sinking his ship as she watched it approach the coast off Bamburgh. The ship landed at Budle Bay and the Childe Wynde walked the short distance to the crags. As he approached, the serpent came out of its lair and went to attack him, but then said…

O quit thy sword, unbend thy brow
And give me kisses three;
For though I be a laidley worm
No harm I'll do to thee.

He duly did as he was told and she then transformed back into the beautiful princess! The happy brother and sister returned to the castle and, drawing on some of her magic, turned the wicked stepmother into an ugly toad!

Now on the sand near Ida's tower
She crawls a loathsome toad

And venom spits on every maid
She meets upon the road

The story of the Laidley Worm is one of several 'worm' legends throughout Northumbria, which probably have their origins in the pagan stories of pre-Conquest Britain. The 'spindlestone' was a slender stone to which the Childe Wynd tied his horse as he approached the lair of the worm, whilst near to the road is an small hollow of marshy ground known as Laidley Worm's Trough. The crags of Spindlestone Heughs rise high above the small wooded valley of Waren Burn (pronounced 'wear-un'), which begins life as a peaty burn on Chatton Moor several miles to the south-west. This stream has carved quite a steep-sided valley in places, often cloaked in deciduous woodland, before it eventually drains into the sea at Budle Bay, a vast expanse of mudflats and sandbanks protected as a National Nature Reserve. Our route passes an old watermill set in a hollow along the wooded banks of Waren Burn, above which to the west is Spindlestone Ducket, a tall and slender stone windmill that dates from the late 18th Century, built on the site of an earlier fortified manor farmhouse; the sails have long since disappeared. There has been a village at Spindlestone since medieval times when it was considerably larger than the small hamlet of today. A footpath leads alongside the thickly wooded Waren Burn passing through the hamlet of Bradford, derived from 'broad ford' that once crossed the Waren Burn.

LUCKER stands astride Waren Burn, which flows through the heart of this pleasant village. The name 'lucker' is said to be derived from the Old Norse words meaning a 'marsh frequented by sandpipers', indeed, much of the surrounding area was little more than boggy marshland until it was drained in the 19th Century. In medieval times, Lucker was quite a sizeable village with several cottages and farms, a mill and a chapel; there are well preserved medieval ridge and furrow ploughing strips in many of the surrounding fields. St Hilda's Church stands on the site of a medieval chapel, although the present church dates from the 1870's when the Duke of Northumberland rebuilt much of the village, which still forms part of the Duke's vast Northumberland Estates. St

Hilda's is a delightful church set on a gently sloping bank above the wooded Waren Burn, with a double bell-cote and distinctive apse at its east end. Just up from the church in the centre of the road junction is the village War Memorial, dedicated to the brave young local men *"who gave their lives in defence of righteousness and freedom in the Great War."* Beside the traditional village 'local', which also serves as the Post Office, stands the Old Mill. This old three-storey corn mill was built in the 18th Century on the site of an earlier mill; it is now used as holiday cottages. Between Lucker and Warenford the footpath leads up along the edge of the steep-sided and thickly wooded banks of Waren Burn, known locally along this stretch as Howe Water, above which are the remains of a large Iron Age camp and fort on its north bank.

WARENFORD developed around the old fording point of the Great North Road across the Waren Burn, as the name suggests. The ford was replaced long ago by a bridge - the present bridge in the heart of the village dates from the late Georgian period, although this has since been by-passed by a more modern road-bridge. The first reference to Warenford was in medieval times when it appears to have been a much busier place than today with a chapel, mill, several more cottages and a leper hospital dedicated to St John the Baptist; no trace remains of this hospital. A former gatehouse in the centre of the village watches over the old driveway that leads up to Twizell House. This house was once the home of renowned ornithologist Prideaux John Selby, whose most celebrated work was Illustrations of British Ornithology, completed in 1834. Selby was also a keen gardener with a special interest in the cultivation of trees. He gained a great deal of his knowledge from the extensive plantations he created around the house and estate, which he later used to compile another of his celebrated works, entitled History of British Forest Trees. The large early 19th Century house that belonged to the Selby family was demolished in the 1950's and replaced by the present house, however, the original walled gardens remain. *"Much of the beauty of the grounds around the hall is due to his taste in planting. The romantic little dene, through which the pretty Waren Burn tumbles fantastically, is overhung with trees, and well set with flowers and shrubs."* **(W. W. Tomlinson 'Comprehensive Guide to Northumberland' 1888).**

CHATTON MOOR forms part of the central range of sandstone hills that sweep in a broad arc through the heart of Northumberland, a natural upland barrier between the flat coastal plain and the lush vales on the eastern fringes of the Cheviot Hills. From their northernmost point to the north-west of Belford, where they are known as the Kyloe Hills, these heather-clad moors swing southwards forming a series of ridges and broad swathes of heather moorland including Chatton Moor, Bewick Moor and Alnwick Moor before curving west to form the Rothbury Terraces, Simonside Hills and Harbottle Hills. These hills are known as the 'Black Lands' due to their acidic peaty soils and heather moorland vegetation covering the underlying Fell Sandstone rocks which contrast starkly with the 'White Lands' of the Cheviot Hills, characterised by their broad domed hills cloaked in tough blanched mat-grass. The Black Lands have their own distinctive character with broad moorland ridges that shelve gently towards the coastal plain whilst their western slopes rise sharply with steep escarpments and rocky outcrops facing the Cheviots. Despite their modest height, these beautiful and often over-looked swathes of moorland display all of the landscape, terrain and feel of rugged upland fells and offer superb views in all directions. These sandstone hills are littered with some of the finest examples of prehistoric archaeology in the country ranging from cairns, standing stones and burial cists to hill-forts, settlements, enclosures and the famous cup and ring marked rocks that date back to the Stone Age. There are remains of a stone circle, enclosure and an area of cairn burials on the gently shelving flanks of Whinny Hill whilst, overlooking Mill Burn to the west of Shielhope, are the earthworks of an Iron Age hill-fort. Interestingly, the wide drive our route crosses just above Shielhope was built in 1872 for the visit of the Prince of Wales who stayed at nearby Chillingham Castle, historic home of the Earls of Tankerville (relations of the Grey family) since the 12th Century. This private drive was constructed with a gentle gradient as it was thought that the surrounding roads were too steep for the Royal carriage and horses, thus allowing easier access up onto the moors for a spot of hunting and shooting! The descent from the old abandoned farm of Brownridge down to Chatton Bridge is superb with the rounded

Cheviot Hills, including Hedgehope and The Cheviot itself, rising and falling on the horizon. Incidentally, The Cheviot is pronounced 'chee-viot'. The village of Chatton lies in the broad green valley of the River Till, which actually begins life as the River Breamish on the upper flanks of Cairn Hill high on the Border Ridge. This river then tumbles through the remote Breamish Valley before flowing out into a broad vale where the sandstone hills of the Black Lands block its progress, forcing it northwards skirting Chatton before meandering north across the Milfield Plain to swell the waters of the River Tweed. The River Breamish changes its name to the Till at Bewick Bridge beside an old mill, several miles to the south of Chatton: *Foot of Breamish and head of Till, Meet together at Bewick Mill.*

CHATTON is one of the prettiest villages in Northumberland with attractive stone cottages centred on a small triangular green. Many of these cottages were built by the Duke of Northumberland for his estate workers, including a particularly fine row of early 19th Century single-storey Tudor-style cottages. The village still forms part of the Duke of Northumberland's estates. Chatton is quite a thriving place that has not lost its soul as a commuter or retirement village and still boasts a school, Post Office and traditional village shop (note the early 19th Century blacksmith's shop next door), art gallery housed in the old Presbyterian church, a Wildlife in Need Sanctuary and, of course, the comfortable Percy Arms Hotel at the heart of the community, which was originally built as a hunting lodge for the Duchess in the early 19th Century. The village 'spirit' is partly due to the fact that Chatton stands as one of the few villages in the central sandstone hills. Its quiet streets and attractive cottages belie a turbulent past for Chatton once lay on the route of invading armies - both English and Scottish - and was frequently terrorised during the Middle Ages by Scottish raiders as well as soldiers from both sides of the Border seeking to replenish their supplies after battle. In response to this threat two defensive pele towers were built in the village; one was situated on Grieve's Law immediately to the north of the village and the other was built beside the old church at the bottom end of the village. This Vicar's Pele Tower was all but demolished during the mid 19th Century when it was incorporated into a more 'modern' Victorian vicarage, designed by the famous Tyneside architect John Dobson. Sadly, no trace of either pele tower remains. *"Edward the First was here for a short time during those critical campaigns when the whole future of Scotland, perhaps, hung on the measure of his waning days, and the pele tower in which the Chatton vicars of the fifteenth century were compelled to entrench themselves is embodied in the present parsonage."* **(A. G. Bradley 1908).** The rather plain 18th Century Holy Cross Church stands beside this Victorian vicarage. There has been a church on this site since the 12th Century when it was granted by William de Vescy, Lord of Alnwick, to the Premonstratensian monks of Alnwick Abbey with whom it remained until the Dissolution of the Monasteries, after which the patronage passed to the Earls of Northumberland. This Norman church fell into ruin and was rebuilt in the 1770's, with later additions during the 19th Century; the church has a rather unusual tower with its bell hanging halfway up the tower wall. In 1814 a discovery was made on the north side of the churchyard of a large stone coffin, inside which were the remains of a man who had died in 1318 whilst on a campaign through Northumberland with Robert Bruce - the coffin also contained a silver penny from the period as well as a steel spur and remains of his helmet.

Chatton

FOWBERRY TOWER stands amidst beautiful landscaped parkland beside the River Till. The history of this fine mansion house dates back to at least the 15th Century when a pele tower was built beside the old ford across the river. As the threat from Scottish raiders and the Border Reivers diminished, this defensive tower house was rebuilt in 1666 to create a larger and more comfortable house, which was almost entirely rebuilt again in the 1770's when it was bought by Sir Francis Blake, a member of a wealthy and influential local family. The fine tiers of Gothic lancet windows on its north frontage date from this period. *"Fowberry Tower, built in 1666 as its foundation stone says by "Squire John Strother and Mary his ladye", but much altered by Blakes and Culleys, who made it into one of the finest surviving pieces of Georgian Gothick in the North: not a "sham castle" but an English gentleman's house."* **(Herbert Honeyman 'Northumberland' 1949).** It was once the home of Matthew Culley who, along with his brother George, helped revolutionise agriculture in the late 18th and early 19th Centuries through the selective breeding of livestock (they developed the Border Leicester breed of sheep) as well as the pioneering use of new varieties of cereals, crop rotation and soil cultivation. They were great reformers at the forefront of the agricultural revolution; there is a memorial to Matthew Culley in the church at Chatton. The Culleys made alterations to the house in the early 1800's when they also built the elegant bridge across the Till. *"Fowberry Bridge is a graceful stone structure of two slender arches. The smaller arch, of 1769, spans the drive leading to Fowberry Tower, while the other one, across the Till, was added by Matthew Tulley about 1825 after a young man had been drowned at the dangerous ford."* **(A. Mee 'The King's England: Northumberland' 1952).** The route of the Devil's Causeway, the Roman road from Hadrian's Wall to Tweedmouth, passes to the west of Fowberry, although no remains of this road are visible.

WEETWOOD MOOR stands as a broad ridge of gently rising heather moorland on the western edge of the 'Black Lands' with a steep escarpment that sweeps down towards the flat Milfield Plain to the north of Wooler where the River Glen and Wooler Water flow out from the confines of the Cheviot Hills to swell the waters of the River Till. The descent from this moorland ridge affords a superb panorama of the

Cheviot Hills, whetting your appetite for tomorrow's walk. Weetwood Moor is littered with archaeological remains and stands as one of the finest areas in England for prehistoric rock art, not to mention the many hill-forts, standing stones, field systems and settlements that date back to the Bronze and Iron Age. Many of the sandstone outcrops have the most amazing 'cup and ring' patterns carved onto them. These carvings consist of several concentric rings around a small central hollow, and are as clear and detailed now as when they were carved by Stone Age people some 5,000 years ago. No one really knows the true meaning of these carvings; they could be fertility symbols, religious carvings or perhaps messages for other people travelling through the area as they are usually located on high ground or beside ancient trackways. *"Several of the sandstone rocks on the summit and the higher parts of the hill have been marked by the Celtic inhabitants with those mysterious figures of concentric circles which have puzzled antiquaries so much."* **(W. W. Tomlinson 1888).**

WOOLER is a busy yet functional small town of grey stone buildings set on a hillside above Wooler Water on the very edge of the magnificent Cheviot Hills and the Northumberland National Park. To the north stretches the fertile Milfield Plain, once a vast glacial lake, whilst to the east rise the dark and brooding sandstone hills of central Northumberland. *"The best thing perhaps about Wooler is its position on a hill, with the grey and red roofs, the church rising above them, the little river below and the hills to the west."* **(Nikolaus Pevsner 'The Buildings of England: Northumberland' 1959).** Wooler is a thriving little town that has served this far-flung district of Northumberland, known as Glendale, for centuries and was once famed for its fairs and markets. The name of the town, however, has nothing to do with wool but is derived from the Old English words for stream 'wella' and hill 'law', a reminder of how Wooler has always served the farming communities of both hill and valley. *"Wooler itself is chiefly remarkable for its annual fair, an event of such importance that the countryside folk date their doings from it, whatever happens being so long from or so long to Wooler Fair."* **(J. S. Fletcher 'The Enchanting North' 1908).** People have been living in this area from the earliest times, the evidence of which lies preserved across the surrounding hills including dozens of Bronze Age burial sites, Iron Age forts and field systems as well as an important Saxon Royal palace! Just to the west of Wooler, on the northernmost edge of the Cheviots, is the distinctive hill of Yeavering Bell crowned by the remains of the largest Iron Age hill-fort in the county that dates back to around 400BC. The hill-fort was abandoned in around 300AD for reasons unknown, although this important site was re-used in Anglo-Saxon times when a large palace known as Ad Gefrin was built just to the north of Yeavering Bell. It grew to be an important Royal township where Edwin, King of Northumbria had one of his palaces in the early 7th Century and where the missionary Paulinus came as his guest in 627AD to baptise many of the local pagans in the River Glen. With the demise of Saxon England, Ad Gefrin all but disappeared and became a place of legend - according to tradition this was where King Arthur fought and won one of his many legendary battles against the invading Anglo-Saxons following which he took control of the Saxon fortress at Bamburgh and gave it to Sir Lancelot who named it 'Din Guardi'. Interestingly, both the names 'Yeavering Bell' and 'Gefrin' mean the 'hill of the goats'; wild goats still roam the Cheviot Hills to this day. Following the Norman Conquest, this area formed the heart of a barony given by Henry I to the Muschampe family. They soon built a castle on a strategic promontory above Humbleton Burn just to the west of present-day Wooler, which consisted of a wooden tower and buildings surrounded by a palisade and defensive ditch. The earthworks of this castle, known as Green Castle although referred to locally as the 'cup and saucer', can still be seen and stand as a good example of a Ringwork castle so named due to its distinctive shape. Wooler soon developed into an important trading centre and was granted a licence to hold a weekly market and regular fairs in 1199; by the 13th Century it was a major centre for the wool trade and became one of Northumberland's most important towns. Unfortunately, the growing threat from the Scots as well as the Border Reivers tempered this growth somewhat and the original Norman castle was abandoned sometime in the 14th Century, later replaced by a defensive stone pele tower in the centre of the developing market town, although some historians claim that this was the site of Wooler's original castle. Built about 1500, this stout tower formed part of a chain of defences across the Border region against the Scots, who plundered the town on several occasions most notably in 1340 and 1409. Known locally as the Tory, the scant remains of this tower can still be seen on the grassy promontory of Tower Hill off Church Street; the three remaining large blocks of masonry are scattered around a beautifully carved War Memorial cross. This whole area suffered at the hands of Scottish and English armies for many centuries and witnessed several notable battles including the Battle of Homildon Hill that was fought in the fields below Humbleton Hill in 1402 when the Scots lost most of their gentry and over a thousand soldiers to the superior English army under the command of Harry 'Hotspur' Percy; this battle was immortalised in Shakespeare's Henry IV. The Battle of Flodden, one of the most famous and bloodiest battles fought during the Border Troubles, took place a few miles further north in 1513, which resulted in the death of James IV of Scotland, most of his nobles and 10,000 Scottish soldiers at the hands of the English army under the command of the Earl of Surrey; James IV was the last British monarch to die in battle. In 1715 the Northumbrian Jacobite rebels under the command of the hapless General Forster and the Earl of Derwentwater stayed in Wooler overnight on their way south to proclaim James Stuart as rightful king. As the Border Troubles slowly came to an end, Wooler prospered as a thriving trading centre, a role it continues to this day. The arrival of the Turnpike road through Wooler during the mid 18th Century was the catalyst for change and marked a period of growth for the town with several coaching inns opening their doors including the Black Bull Hotel, Red Lion and the Cottage Hotel, now known as the Tankerville Arms, plus several more inns that have long since disappeared. The Alnwick to Cornhill Railway came through Wooler in 1887 bringing with it a pulse of life and providing a valuable route to market for local produce and livestock; the line closed in 1965 and the old stone-built station can still be seen just off South Road. Wooler was all but destroyed by two devastating fires that swept through the town in 1722 and, particularly, 1863 when virtually every building along the High Street and Market Place was destroyed; one of the few buildings to survive was the Angel Inn, a rare example of Georgian architecture.

This explains the uniform design of houses, shops and pubs along the High Street, many of which have retained their original Victorian frontages including Hamish Dunn 'Antiques and Curios', although the etched glass door of this shop proclaims that it was once the home of J. Pringle & Co, Boot and Shoe Manufacturers. St Mary's Church stands proudly in the centre of Wooler, built in 1765 in local sandstone on the site of a 12th Century thatched church that was destroyed by the fire of 1722. It was during the Georgian and Victorian eras that Wooler grew as a health resort with 'invalids' attracted by the magnificent countryside and fresh mountain air, although part of the 'cure' including drinking goat's whey! Grace Darling stayed here when she was suffering from TB during the last few weeks of her short life. Wooler was also the birthplace of the famous Dalziel brothers - George, Edward, John and Thomas - who became famous in Victorian times for their wood engravings that were used as illustrations in many magazines, periodicals and books including Punch, The Illustrated London News and Alice in Wonderland. *"Wooler is such a town as you would expect to see in the heart of the county, decidedly rustic, with roofs of thatch here and there to temper aspiring notions, with shops that remind you of the days of George III., but yet with indications of homely prosperity. The parson preached in a thatched church till it was burnt down about a hundred years ago. With two thousand inhabitants it is an important metropolis, drawing folk to its fairs and markets from miles around, and, as I saw, careful to send its boys and girls to school."* **(Walter White 'Northumberland and The Border' 1859).** Today, Wooler is a pleasant old market town that still serves the far-flung district of Glendale, and is busy in summer with visitors who use the town as a base to explore the magnificent surrounding countryside. The Glendale district covers almost 250 square miles of North Northumberland and has one of the smallest populations in the country - just 24 people per square mile. It was the sparsely populated rolling green hills and wide valleys of this area that provided the inspiration for the popular children's story 'Postman Pat' as well as the fictional village of Greendale. The author of the stories, John Cuncliffe, operated the Wooler Mobile Library during the 1950's.

STAGE FIVE

WOOLER
to
ALWINTON

✦

"From the remote farmhouse of Alnhammoor, I followed a wide grassy path skirting across the flanks of Shill Moor, a clearly discernable ribbon of darker green snaking its way through a landscape of rounded hills, bleached grass and far horizons; this is the 'White Lands' at the very heart of the lonely Cheviot Hills. The ever-changing view provided a frequent respite from the gradual climb up to join the Salter's Road, an old green lane across the hills that was once busy with packhorses and merchants plying their trade between the coast and Scotland. Then there was nothing; nothing but the faint sound of my heart beating and the gentle breeze, the distant bleat of sheep and the evocative cry of a curlew. Nothing but the soft sound of the hills. There are few places left in England where you can truly find solitude and wilderness; the Cheviot Hills are once such place."

Mark Reid
July 2003

WALK INFORMATION

Points of interest:	A wishing well, in the shadow of Hedgehope Hill, Langlee and Housey Crags, a mystical stone circle, isolated farmsteads and ancient settlements, the beautiful Breamish Valley, the road paved with salt, a hidden fortified chapel, and the magnificent Cheviot Hills.
Distance:	Wooler to Greensidehill Farm 10.5 miles Greensidehill Farm to Alwinton 10 miles Total 20.5 miles
Time	Allow 8 - 9 hours
Facilities:	There are no facilities along this walk - take sufficient food, water and provisions with you. This walk does, however, pass several isolated farmhouses.
Terrain:	*NB: This walk heads through remote countryside with few landmarks, which may make navigation difficult in poor weather - take a compass and OS map with you on this walk.* From Wooler, clear field paths lead across Wooler Common to join a quiet country lane which is then followed for about 3 miles up into the Harthope Valley, although 1.5 miles of this road is unenclosed with Access Land on either side. A grassy bridleway (boggy in places) is joined at Langlee, which climbs steadily up passing between Langlee Crags and Housey Crags over into Threestoneburn Wood from where a stony track leads down to The Dod (farm). Grassy paths head south from The Dod over into the Breamish Valley - the path on the ground is

clear for most of the way and is marked by waymarkers, with only one or two indistinct sections. From the Breamish Valley, a clear grassy path heads up to join the Salter's Road (grassy track) which is followed to Ewartly Shank Farm from where narrow footpaths lead south across grassy moorland of Hazeltonrig Hill and Sing Moor to Biddlestone - the path on the ground is indistinct in places, although waymarking is generally good. From Biddlestone, quiet country lanes and old tracks lead through woodland and across pastureland all the way to Alwinton.

| Ascents: | Langlee Crags: | 385 metres |
| | Little Dod: | 380 metres |

Viewpoints: River scenery alongside Harthope Burn.
Views across towards The Cheviot and Hedgehope Hill on the ascent from Langlee over towards Threestoneburn House.
Descent into the Breamish Valley from The Dod.
Views across Shank Burn from Little Dod.
Views across Coquetdale during the descent to Biddlestone.

FACILITIES

Wooler	Inn / B&B / Shop / P.O. / Café / Bus / Phone / Toilets / Info / YH / Camp
Middleton Hall	Phone
Biddlestone	Phone
Alwinton	Inn / B&B / P.O. / Café / Bus / Phone / Toilets

ROUTE DESCRIPTION

(Map Seventeen)

From the Market Place in the centre of Wooler, walk up along Ramsey's Lane (SP 'Wooler Common') and follow this up then levelling out heading out of the town. Just before the houses end on your right, take the track branching off up to the left (SP 'Wooler Common'). Follow this track on to reach a bridle-gate just beyond Waud House, after which follow the grassy path to the left (SP 'Pin Well') that leads on with marshy ground to your right at first then along the bottom of a dry valley before it drops down passing the 'Pin Well' on your right to reach a gate across your path. Head straight on along the clear track to reach a junction with an old quarry lane, where you turn right down to reach the road. Turn right along the road and follow this on to reach the hamlet of Earle after about 0.25 miles. Walk through the hamlet, following the road as it bends to the left after the small 'green' (SP 'Middleton Hall, Langleeford') and continue straight on along the road (ignore the turning to the left), passing Walker Walls Cottages on to reach the hamlet of Middleton Hall. Take the turning to the right beside the Victorian Post-box (SP 'Langleeford') and follow this climbing steeply up (1-in-5 gradient) through woodland. The road levels out after about 0.25 miles, then drops down to reach Skirl Naked farm and a cattle grid across the road (National Park boundary). Carry straight on along the road dropping steeply down to reach Carey Burn Bridge - continue on along this road (unenclosed for much of the way) with Harthope Burn to your left for a further 1.25 miles until you reach a turning to the left over a large bridge towards Langlee Farm (the first farm you come to along the valley). Head left along this track (SP 'Threestoneburn House, The Dod, Ilderton Moor') over the bridge, immediately after which take the grassy track to the right (do not head up towards Langlee Farm). Follow this grassy track on through a gate, after which continue straight on along the gently rising track across the top of The Shank (small ridge of land), with Harthope Burn down to your right and Leech Burn to your left, then follow the track as it bends round to the left passing a stone sheepfold then climbs steeply uphill, with the deep cleft of Wester Dean across to your left. The grassy path bears gradually to the right up across the hillside to join a stone wall on your right, which you follow up to reach a clear shooters' track across your path (Langlee Crags across to your left and Housey Crags across to your right) and a gate to your right (where the stone wall ends and fence begins). Turn right along this track over the stile beside the gate.

(Map Eighteen)

After the gate, turn immediately left along a wide path (do not head along the shooters' track). Follow this clear grassy path straight on across the grassy / heather moorland gradually bearing away from the fence, then gradually drop down passing the outcrops of Tathey Crags across to your right to reach a large black shed (sheep food store). Continue straight on along the grassy path passing this shed to reach a bridle-gate that leads into Threestoneburn Wood (large plantation). Follow the wide track through the forest down to reach a bridle-gate / stile at the end of the forest that leads out into a large clearing (short detour to Threestoneburn stone circle to the right before this gate). Follow the path straight on heading towards Threestoneburn House hidden in the trees, over two small footbridges then over another stile / bridle-gate after which head on over a large FB then bear left passing to the side of Threestoneburn House then on across the yard to join a clear track. Follow this track straight on for just over a mile to reach The Dod (farm). As you approach the large barn (approx. 500 yards before it) with the small plantation ahead of you to the right, turn right over a stile then left across the field over another stile that leads through the middle of the plantation. Head straight on through the dense trees to quickly emerge with the farm buildings of The Dod ahead of you, where you turn right passing the farmhouse down along a track to reach a gate beside the corner of the plantation on your right. After the gate, follow the clear grassy track straight on over a small bridge over Harelaw Burn after which continue along the track bearing slightly round to the right (waymarker) then straight on along the grassy track running parallel to the fence to your right (ignore the gate in this fence) across the gently sloping hillside. After a while the track disappears - continue straight on (waymarker) gradually bearing to the right to join the fence-line on your right which you follow straight on to reach a gate across your path. Head through the gate then carry straight on alongside the fence climbing steadily up to the top of the small hill, at the top of which you reach a junction of paths by a gate on your right (waymarker). Continue straight on across the rough grassy hillside (no clear path - head towards the gate in the distance on top of the next low 'rise' of moorland) slanting very slightly down across the gently sloping hillside to reach some old sheep enclosures (corrugated metal) in an area of grass on the edge of the heather moorland at the bottom of the gentle slope. Carry straight on passing immediately to the left of these old enclosures across heather moorland to soon join a wide grassy bridleway (waymarker) which you follow straight on up to reach a stile beside a gate across your path. After the gate, follow the path to the right to quickly join a wide grassy path (waymarker) which you follow straight on passing to the right of a section of stone wall to reach a gate across your path. Head through the gate then, after about 200 yards, the bridleway divides (Cunyan Crags up to your right) - bear to the left along the clear grassy bridleway gently heading down across the hillside (ignore grassy tracks across your path) to reach the earthworks and overgrown enclosures of a deserted medieval village. As you reach the edge of the deserted village, follow the path to the right (waymarker) then straight on heading very gradually down across the gently sloping hillside, over three footbridges across small tributaries of Willow Burn then straight on down to join a grassy path (about 200 yards below a large pile of boulders) at the head of the small valley of Willow Burn. Head left along this grassy path down across a ford over Willow Burn then follow the clear path round to the left (waymarker) then straight on across the right-hand side of the small valley to join a stone wall on your right that quickly leads to a bridle-gate in a fence across your path. Drop down passing to the left of Greensidehill Farm to reach a bridle-gate (SP) that leads onto the road. Turn right along the road passing in front of Greensidehill Farm and follow this road climbing up then levelling out on to reach the next farmhouse at Hartside (ignore the lane to the left just before this farm).

Immediately after the farm buildings, take the FP to the left through a gate (SP 'Alnhammoor') and bear to the right across the field to reach a bridle-gate towards the bottom right corner that leads onto a unenclosed lane. Follow this lane to the right down over a bridge across the River Breamish then up towards Alnhammoor Farm.

(Map Nineteen)

As the lane bends to the right just before Alnhammoor Farm take the FP to the left over a stile beside a gate, then straight across the field (with the farmhouse up to your right) through another gate and onto a track. Turn right along this track then, just after you have passed the stone barn behind the farmhouse, head straight on bearing slightly to the left along a narrow grassy path that leads across the top of a small bank (Shank Burn down to your left) to reach a ladder stile over a fence across your path. After the stile, head down over a small FB across Rowhope Burn then follow the clear grassy track straight on (waymarker). Continue along the clear grassy path as it gently rises up then gradually bears away from Shank Burn (and its distinctive U-shaped valley) climbing up across the grassy hillside (waymarkers) to reach a stile / gate in a fence across your path. After the gate, carry on along the wide grassy path (do not follow the fence-line) heading up across the hillside, which levels out for a while passing to the right of an old stone sheepfold, then climbs up bearing slightly to the left across the 'shoulder' of Shill Moor. The path levels out and heads on skirting across the flanks Shill Moor to reach the grassy track of Salter's Road across your path (waymarker) overlooking the valley of Smalehope Burn (actually the upper reaches of Shank Burn). Turn left along Salter's Road (grassy track) and follow it as it rises up over Little Dod then drops down into the valley of Shank Burn before a final steep descent to reach a FB across the stream. After the stream follow the grassy track climbing quite steeply up out of the valley to reach a stile / gate at the corner of a plantation. Follow the path through the forest to quickly emerge out onto a field, then head straight on towards Ewartly Shank farm. Skirt to the right around the barns, just after which head left through a gate that leads into the farmyard then, immediately before the farmhouse, head to the right off the track (SP) over two stiles and out onto a field. Head straight on bearing slightly to the left across the rough field to reach a stile over a fence (about 200 yards to the left of the stone sheepfold / bottom of the narrow plantation), after which head on across boggy ground bearing slightly to the right (waymarkers) to join a fence on your right which you follow up through a gate across your path to reach an unenclosed road by a cattle grid (SP). Head right along the road over the cattle grid, just after which turn right along the clear grassy path (SP 'Biddlestone') then, after about 25 yards, head to the left along an indistinct narrow path (waymarkers) across grassy moorland (do not follow the clearer path heading up the hillside). Follow this narrow path straight on across the flanks of the gently sloping hillside (waymarkers) to reach a gate in a fence across your path just before the Tod Stones (outcrops) above the ravine of Hogdonlaw Sike. Follow the path between the rocks then down over the stream (above a waterfall) then up the other side (take care) after which head on across the hillside passing through the site of an ancient farmstead then carry straight on bearing very slightly to the right across the gently sloping hillside (no clear path), over a small stream then bear to the left (waymarker) to reach a stile over a fence. After the stile, head right (passing concrete foundations of a building) and follow the narrow path across the hillside (waymarkers) to soon join a clearer grassy track. Follow this track straight on then, where two plantations come into view and the grassy track curves round to the right, head straight on off this track (waymarker) across rough ground heading towards the top right end of the long plantation ahead of you. As you approach this plantation, drop down over a stream then up to a stile that leads into the forest (about 100 yards from the top right end), then bear to the right through the dense trees to quickly reach a stile at the end of the plantation. Head to the right across the field passing the corner of the plantation then continue on to reach a stile over the fence about 50 yards down from the end of the plantation (ignore the stile / gate beside the plantation). After the stile head up to quickly join a wide grassy path (this path originates from the stile / gate beside the plantation), and follow this clear path to the left heading across the hillside through bracken and heather with the small valley of Harden Burn down to your left on to join a clearer track that leads down to reach a gate just above the stream. Head through the gate, over the ford across the stream then follow the track up to reach two gates - head through the right-hand gate and follow the grassy track up (with the stream down to your right) to join a clear red stony track. Follow this track straight on dropping quite steeply down (views of Simonside ahead) then, where the track bends round to the right and levels out, cross the stile / bridlegate to the left (do not continue along the track). Head straight down across the field to reach a stile beside a gate that leads onto the road, then follow this road to the right to reach a junction beside the 'phone box at Biddlestone (Quarry entrance to your right) where you turn left to quickly reach another road junction.

(Map Twenty)

At the junction, turn right and follow the road on over a bridge across Biddlestone Burn just after which take the track to the right (SP) through a gate into the forest. Immediately after the gate take the path to the right (waymarker) and follow the narrow path meandering through the trees to reach Biddlestone Chapel set in a small clearing. Pass to the right of the Chapel, after which head to the left around the Chapel back into the forest (waymarker), following the path bending initially to the right then straight on through the dense trees to reach a track across your path. Turn left along this track down to reach the road. Turn right along the road and follow this on for approx. 0.5 miles then, where the road bends sharp left, continue straight on along the track ahead (SP 'Clennell'). Follow this clear track straight on (ignore the track to the right up to Rookland Farm) heading through a series of gates, becoming a grassy track after a while. The track continues straight on down through a plantation then emerges with Clennell Cottages across to your right (red stony track) - carry straight on along this track then where it bends to the right and crosses the small stream head straight on through the gate in the stone wall ahead that leads into the caravan park. Head straight on to quickly join a track which you follow through the caravan park (keeping close to the fence on your left) then, at the end of this field where it joins another track, head straight on away from these tracks along the grassy path ahead (with Clennell Hall across to your right) through the main entrance gates to the Hall and onto a lane. Turn right then almost immediately left over a FB (SP 'Alwinton), after which follow the path to the left up a bank to reach a stile then head straight across two fields to reach the enclosed track of Clennell Street. Turn left and follow this track down into Alwinton.

Wooler

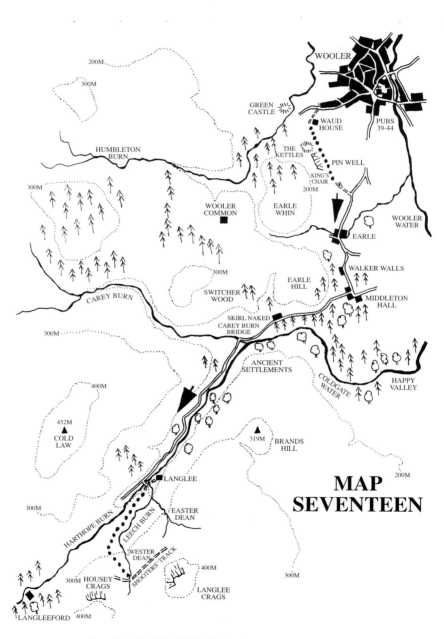

MAP
SEVENTEEN

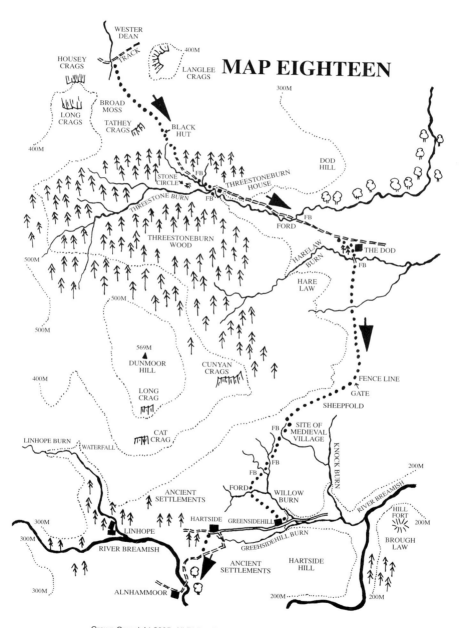

MAP EIGHTEEN

WESTER DEAN

HOUSEY CRAGS

400M

LANGLEE CRAGS

BROAD MOSS

LONG CRAGS

TATHEY CRAGS

400M

TRACK

BLACK HUT

300M

DOD HILL

STONE CIRCLE

FB

THREESTONEBURN HOUSE

THREESTONE BURN

FB

FORD

FB

THREESTONEBURN WOOD

HARELAW BURN

THE DOD

FB

500M

HARE LAW

500M

500M

569M
DUNMOOR HILL

CUNYAN CRAGS

LONG CRAG

400M

FENCE LINE

GATE

SHEEPFOLD

CAT CRAG

SITE OF MEDIEVAL VILLAGE

FB

LINHOPE BURN

WATERFALL

FB

FB

KNOCK BURN

200M

FORD

WILLOW BURN

RIVER BREAMISH

ANCIENT SETTLEMENTS

HARTSIDE

GREENSIDEHILL

HILL FORT

200M

LINHOPE

300M

300M

RIVER BREAMISH

GREENSIDEHILL BURN

BROUGH LAW

ANCIENT SETTLEMENTS

HARTSIDE HILL

300M

ALNHAMMOOR

200M

200M

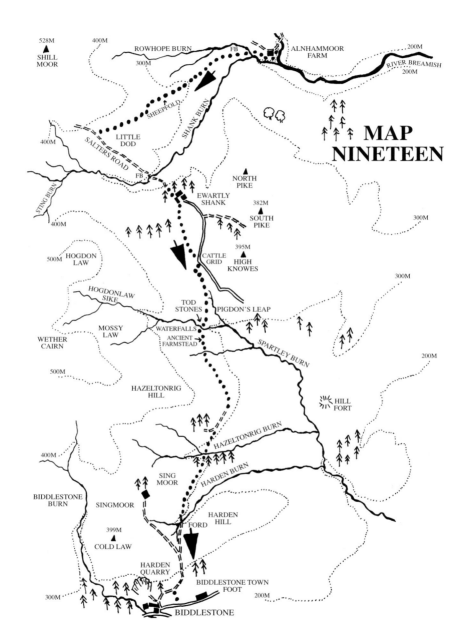

MAP
NINETEEN

528M
SHILL MOOR
400M
ROWHOPE BURN
FB
ALNHAMMOOR FARM
200M
RIVER BREAMISH
200M
300M
SHANK BURN
SHEEPFOLD
LITTLE DOD
400M
SALTERS ROAD
FB
STING BURN
400M
EWARTLY SHANK
NORTH PIKE
382M
SOUTH PIKE
300M
CATTLE GRID
395M
HIGH KNOWES
HOGDON LAW
500M
HOGDONLAW SIKE
TOD STONES
PIGDON'S LEAP
300M
MOSSY LAW
WETHER CAIRN
WATERFALLS
ANCIENT FARMSTEAD
SPARTLEY BURN
200M
500M
HAZELTONRIG HILL
HILL FORT
HAZELTONRIG BURN
400M
SING MOOR
HARDEN BURN
BIDDLESTONE BURN
SINGMOOR
399M
COLD LAW
FORD
HARDEN HILL
HARDEN QUARRY
BIDDLESTONE TOWN FOOT
300M
200M
BIDDLESTONE

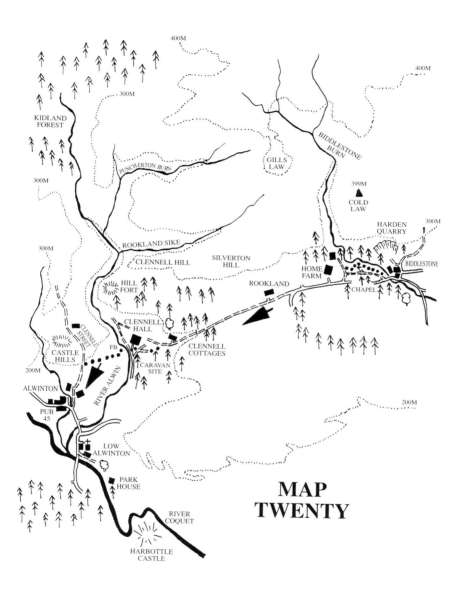

MAP
TWENTY

THE PIN WELL lies to the west of the town, hidden away in a steep-sided dry valley that was scoured out by glacial meltwaters towards the end of the last Ice Age. This small natural spring is protected by a rough border of stones, its crystal clear waters flowing out to form an area of boggy ground near the bottom of the valley. In times past, local people would walk to this well on May Day each year and throw a bent pin into the water and then make a wish. The well was said to be the home of a fairy who would then grant them their wish before the end of the year. Such was the popularity of this wishing well that it became somewhat of a ritual for people attending the famous Wooler fairs to walk the short distance from the town to throw in their bent pins! Such customs and beliefs stem from the pagan practice of well-worshipping as our prehistoric ancestors would have thought these clear, unpolluted springs rising straight out of the ground to be quite miraculous. Above the crags on the western side of the valley are the earthworks of a large Iron Age fort and settlement known as The Kettles that was built by the native British Votadini tribe who occupied this area over 2,000 years ago. At the bottom edge of this fort, just above the Pin Well, is a large seat-like rock called the King's Chair where, according to legend, a long-forgotten king of the ancient Celtic people sat whilst directing the proceedings of a raging battle in the valley below!

EARLE, also known by its old name of Yearle, is a delightful hamlet of well-kept cottages and farm buildings set around a compact triangular green complete with a small stream. Above the village on the slopes of Earle Whin are the remains of ancient cultivation terraces that possibly date back to prehistoric times. The village of Earle was first mentioned in medieval times when it was much larger than today, indeed, in the late medieval period there was a bastle house at Earle, built in response to the threat from across the Border as well as the notorious Reivers; such defensive farmhouses were only built by relatively wealthy farmers who had something worth protecting. No trace of this bastle remains.

MIDDLETON HALL stands sentinel at the foot of the narrow country lane that winds its way up into the beautiful Harthope Valley at the very heart of the Cheviot Hills. This small hamlet is actually one of six settlements called 'middleton' in the vicinity, including the deserted medieval village of Middleton Old Town just to the south across the delightfully named Happy Valley. This thickly wooded valley is a popular local beauty spot where Harthope Burn, although still referred to by its old name of Coldgate Water, meanders through a narrow valley emerging from the foothills of the Cheviots before curving northwards, and changing its name once again to Wooler Water, towards Milfield Plain. In medieval times, the hamlet of Middleton Hall would have also been a larger settlement as early records show that there were two bastle houses here, although no trace of either defensive building remains. These records refer to the Old Hall at Middleton, which once formed part of the estates of the influential Derwentwater family who forfeited much of their property following their involvement with the ill-fated 1715 Jacobite Uprising. The Old Hall probably incorporated one of these bastle houses and has long since vanished, replaced by the new Middleton Hall, a fine early 19th Century house set amongst beautiful wooded parkland. From Middleton Hall, a narrow road climbs steeply up to the farm at Skirl Naked on the edge of the National Park, from where there is a steep descent to Carey Burn Bridge with the full glory of the Cheviots unfolding with every step. *"As you are dropping down into the valley beyond Middleton, the hills through which your path lies group themselves finely in ascending ridges to the two monarchs of the range, Cheviot and Hedgehope – the latter a fine conical peak with a cairn on its point – which, side by side, fill the background with much distinction."* **(A. G. Bradley 'The Romance of Northumberland' 1908).** Skirl Naked is one of several isolated farms with rather unusual names throughout this region including tongue-twisters such as Uswayford, Batailshiel and Blawearie (ask a local how to pronounce these!). Above Skirl Naked, on the flanks of Hart Heugh, are the remains of prehistoric hut circles as well as an old farmhouse known as Switcher that was once the home of a witch!

HARTHOPE BURN rises on the upper flanks of Cairn Hill close to the Border Ridge on the rounded bulk of the Cheviot massif. From these desolate heights, the peaty burn tumbles through an area of wilderness before cascading down the narrow waterfall of Harthope Linn ('linn' is the Scots Gaelic word for a pool or gushing water) to reach the isolated old farmstead at Langleeford Hope, the first sign of civilisation. Formed by a geological fault and smoothed by ice, the dramatic upper reaches of Harthope Burn form a deep bowl between the looming bulks of The Cheviot (815 metres) and Hedgehope (714 metres), two magnificent mountains that dominate the scene. The Cheviot, known locally as Muckle Cheviot, is a great 'whaleback' of granite renowned for its peat-hags and poor views from the summit; the name 'cheviot' is thought to be derived from the old Celtic words meaning 'snow covered ridge'. *"The summit is a desolate-looking tract of treacherous moss-hags and oozy peat-flats, traversed by deep sykes and interspersed with black stagnant pools."* **(William Weaver Tomlinson 'Comprehensive Guide to Northumberland' 1888).** Beyond Langleeford Hope, the river valley changes in character with ancient woodland along the riverbank and steep valley sides crowding in, only occasionally allowing enough space for one or two flat fields, known as 'haughs', along the valley floor and a trio of isolated farms. About a mile and a half downstream from Langleeford Hope is the farm of Langleeford which has a delightful setting beside a ford across the river; the road up the valley ends here. In the 16th Century, Night Watches were posted here to warn of Reivers or Scottish raiders coming down the valley from the Border Ridge. In more peaceful times, Sir Walter Scott stayed here in 1791 whilst visiting the area, where he spent his time fishing, riding, shooting and walking, as well as drinking goat's whey for breakfast! He wrote to a friend *"Behold a letter from the mountains, for I am very snugly settled here, in a farmer's house about six miles from Wooler in the very centre of the Cheviot Hills, in one of the wildest and most romantic situations which your imagination, fertile upon the subject of cottages, ever suggested."* Langlee Farm lies about a mile further down the valley at the foot of the old bridleway that climbs up between Langlee Crags and Housey Crags, a distinctive outcrop of rock that rises up like a small stone fortress high above the valley. From Carey Burn Bridge to Langlee, the unenclosed valley road follows the banks of the sparkling river through a delightful landscape of wild hills dissected by deep side-valleys. The riverbank is thickly wooded with native species such as alder, birch and oak; gnarled and moss-covered, this ancient woodland offers a rare glimpse of how this landscape would have looked thousands of years ago after the ice caps had retreated. *"From Wooler I have a very favourite walk, and that is up the burn to Langleeford. This burn, running between Cheviot and Hedgehope, finds its source away up in the two hills and it has all the freshness and the mystery of a stream that is yet but a little from its birth. Gay and unstained it flows between the grass and bracken of its banks, reflecting slender trees in the golden brown of its peat-coloured depth."* **(Iris Wedgwood 'Northumberland and Durham' 1932).** The bridleway that leads up from Langlee across The Shank, the local name for a ridge of land, passes the site of a medieval shieling that was used by shepherds during the summer months whilst tending their flocks on the high pastures; the present Langlee Farm developed from this temporary settlement. The bridleway steadily climbs up passing between the outcrops of Langlee Crags and Housey Crags, the best examples of 'baked andesite' tors in the Cheviots, then on down towards Threestoneburn Wood passing another tor known as Tathey Crags. 380 million years ago, the Cheviot Hills began to take shape when this whole area was a mass of volcanoes spewing molten rock, ash and lava from deep within the earth. A huge mountain range was created topped by great drifts of lava, known as andesite, which had pushed up under great force through the earth's crust and spread out across the volcanoes. A great 'plug' of molten rock intruded into the very heart of this savage landscape, then cooled to create a central core of granite (the present-day Cheviot massif). As this huge mass of molten granite intruded into the lavas, the intense heat literally baked the adjacent lavas to create a harder ring of 'baked' andesite rock. Almost 400 million years later, this slightly more resistant rock now forms a huge ring of 'tors' around the central granite core. But the great domed hills of the Cheviots we see today are not extinct volcanoes. The thick andesite 'cap' has eroded down over millions of years leaving the granite core of the Cheviot massif surrounded by a thick nutrient-rich layer of soil created from the weathered andesite covering a range of rounded closely-grouped hills. Today, the prominent feature of these hills is grassland of bleached mat-grass and fescue, which gives the whole area its distinctive character - the 'White Lands'.

Housey Crags

THREESTONEBURN STONE CIRCLE lies in a clearing on the edge of the vast coniferous plantation of Threestoneburn Wood that cloaks the lower eastern flanks of Hedgehope. This stone circle is made up of over a dozen granite stones, although only five remain standing. The stones form a large oval over 100-ft across and were placed here during the Bronze Age, perhaps as a religious site in the shadow of The Cheviot and Hedgehope. Just to the north of here are the remains of a large prehistoric settlement consisting of fifteen hut circles beneath the outcrops of Tathey Crags. Maybe this stone circle was constructed by the people living at this site for religious purposes. According to legend, there were only eleven stones in the circle with a 'missing' twelfth lying hidden somewhere close by with a hoard of gold waiting to be discovered beneath. Many years ago, a local farmer went out to try to find this missing stone and buried treasure but unfortunately uncovered two stones, which totalled a rather unlucky thirteen!

RIVER BREAMISH, which is derived from the ancient Celtic words for 'bright water', rises on a remote hillside known as Scotsman's Knowe close to the Border Ridge. For the first few miles, this fast-flowing river tumbles over its rocky bed through a deep valley hemmed in by high, lonely hills to reach the remote farmhouse at Bleakhope, well named indeed. The river then flows in wide sinuous curves through a narrow gorge set between the steep dramatic slopes of High Cantle and Shill Moor before reaching the cluster of cottages at Linhope. The scenery and landscape changes in the middle valley between Linhope and Ingram with flat riverside pastures, wooded burns and the rounded hills of the 'White Lands' rising high above. Few people live in this area now with just a handful of isolated farms dotted alongside the narrow road, but in prehistoric times the population was much greater with many small communities living in defensive settlements and forts high up on the hills. The rough terrain of the Breamish Valley escaped the plough which means that there is an abundance of prehistoric remains ranging from hill-forts to burial mounds, ancient field systems and settlements dating back to the Bronze Age. One of the finest examples of a hill-fort in this area can be found on Brough Law, a massive promontory of land that juts out into the valley just to the east of Greensidehill, with sheer scree slopes tumbling down its north-western flanks. These hill-forts date back some two and a half thousand years, built not only for defence but also for prestige. The Cheviot Hills were of little interest to the Romans and many of these forts and settlements continued to be occupied throughout the Roman period and subsequent Dark Ages with new huts being built within the old walls and boundaries. By the Norman Conquest, many of these old sites had been abandoned in favour of more sheltered valley locations and soon small villages began to develop. Almost all of these medieval villages were deserted many centuries ago; our route passes across the site of the medieval village of Hartside on the flanks of Dunmoor Hill just above Greensidehill Farm. The remains of around fifteen buildings can be clearly seen across the gently shelving hillside as well as preserved banks, ditches and ridge and furrow ploughing strips. There was also a medieval village known as Alnhamsheles on the slopes above Rowhope Burn near the present farmhouse at Alnhammoor. This village was first mentioned in 1265 but was abandoned by the 16th Century; the remains of around twenty huts and buildings have been traced. Incidentally, the words 'law' and 'dun' mean a hill in Old English, whilst 'dod' refers to a rounded hill and 'hope' means a 'narrow strip of fertile land in a valley'.

SALTER'S ROAD has been an important route across the hills since at least the 13th Century; it has been used by Reivers, smugglers, drovers and trains of packhorses carrying loads of salt across the hills up to join the ancient route of Clennell Street on the Border Ridge over into Scotland. Many centuries ago, salt was a valuable commodity used to preserve meat during the winter months and so roads were built to connect the salt-pans along the coast with towns and markets inland. From the Northumberland coast, this old road travelled through Rothbury then on to Alnham on the edge of the Cheviot Hills from where it meandered across the hills up to the Border Ridge; the section from Alnham to the Border survives as a superb green lane through a wonderful landscape beneath the high hills of Hogdon Law, Cushat Law and Bloodybush Edge. Images of packhorses and traders heading across the hills spring to mind as you drop down from Little Dod to the old ford across Shank Burn, although keep an eye on your wallet as this old track was used by smugglers and was also known as Thief's Road! Our route leaves Salter's Road at Ewartly Shank and follows a footpath across the lower flanks of Hogdon Law to reach the delightful Hogdonlaw Sike where it tumbles over a series of small waterfalls beside the outcrops of the Tod Stones. Just down from here is Pigdon's Leap, a narrow ravine along Pigdon's Sike. According to legend, a Border Reiver named Pigdon leapt this chasm on his horse and escaped his pursuers to steal another day!

BIDDLESTONE lies sheltered beneath Cold Law and Bleakmoor Hill, the descent from which is superb with views across the wide wooded vale of Biddlestone Burn towards the flat-topped ridge of the Simonside Hills in the distance. A handful of attractive cottages stand just above the thickly wooded banks of the stream, which changes its name several times en route to swell the waters of the River Coquet at Thropton. Just above the village is Harden Quarry, a sizeable working quarry that scars the southern foothills of the Cheviot Hills. About 300 million years ago a narrow intrusion of magma pushed up through cracks in the overlying andesite layer, in a similar way to the Great Whin Sill, to create a 'laccolith' or dyke of felsite rock. This durable stone with its rich red colour has been quarried for many years and is a highly prized road-stone - 'Harden red' stone chippings are used to surface motorway verges, driveways and lanes throughout the country including The Mall and Buckingham Palace, not to mention local moorland tracks! Hidden away amongst the trees just to the west of the hamlet of Biddlestone is a rather unusual chapel set in a small clearing. The stoutly-built walls and numerous blocked up doorways indicate that there is more to this early 19th Century Roman Catholic chapel than first meets the eye - it is actually built on top of a medieval defensive pele tower! This was originally known as Biddlestone Tower, the historic home of the Selby family who lived at Biddlestone for over six hundred years. Sir Walter de Selby was given lands in this area by Edward I in 1272 due to his loyalty to the English Crown during the Border Troubles, although in later years the Selby family had a tendency to get rather too involved with Border 'affairs' and so regularly had their lands confiscated. *"A brave and warlike race, the Biddleston family were invariably mixed up in all Border troubles, and few of the heads of the house died in their beds. In the great civil war they espoused the cause of Charles I., for which they suffered heavily by fines and sequestrations; and in the Jacobite Rising of 1715 they were found in the thick of it, along with their friends the Collingwoods of Eslington, the Claverings of Callaly, the Talbots of Cartington, and other Northumbrian families."* **(David Dippie Dixon, 'Upper Coquetdale', 1903).** This Tower was later incorporated into a larger manor house, which in turn was replaced by Biddlestone Hall in the late 18th Century, a large three-storey Georgian mansion built immediately to the south of (and adjoining) this old pele tower. The Hall remained in the Selby family until early 20th century and was demolished in the 1950's; all that remains are the crumbling foundations and floor tiles beside the old chapel. As with many notable families in the North of England, the Selbys were staunch Catholics who kept the Old Faith alive in this remote corner of Coquetdale. The Biddle Stones refer to a medieval cross that was either a roadside waymarker or perhaps even a market cross which once stood within the small medieval village of Biddlestone that surrounded Biddlestone Tower; all trace of this village was swept away when the Hall was built. The base of this cross still lies beside the track through the forest leading up to the old chapel. Biddlestone Hall is said to be the Osbaldistone Hall featured in Sir Walter Scott's novel 'Rob Roy', which was published in 1817. *"A mile or so beyond we traversed the grounds of an old country house, which lay back with its encircling woodlands against the Cheviots, and interested me infinitely, that of Biddlestone, still owned by the Selbys. But much more than that, it was also the Osbaldistone Hall of Scott's Rob Roy. Like many other people, no doubt, I had treasured throughout life an Osbaldistone Hall of my own imagining, and I had now to picture Di Vernon galloping over strange pastures, that I am not ashamed to say gave me something of a thrill as I found myself listening for the echo of her horse's hoofs."* **(A. G. Bradley 1908).**

CLENNELL HALL stands strategically at the entrance to the beautiful Alwin Valley, which drains the remote hills of Bloodybush Edge and Cushat Law, although much of its upper reaches are cloaked in coniferous tress that form the extensive Kidland Forest. Clennell Hall was originally a pele tower, built in the 14th Century for the influential Clennell family. In the 1560's, a manor house was built adjoining this pele tower, which stands as a very rare example of an undefended Elizabethan house right in the heart of 'Reivers' country, although some historians believe the house to be of a later date. Both of these early buildings survive, although hidden somewhat by the large Tudor-style house that was built during the 1890's. Clennell, along with neighbouring Biddlestone and Alwinton, was one of the famous 'Ten Towns of Coquetdale' under the control of the Lord of Harbottle Castle which were required to supply men and arms during the Border Troubles. This medieval village was all but cleared away when the large house was built and surrounding parkland laid out during the late 19th Century, which is now used as a caravan site! *"These reasons were given by the people of "Cockdale" in the neighbouring valley, to account for the desolation of Kidland, which lay open on the northward to attacks from the*

Scots, and had no defence on the south from the reivers of Redesdale. The inhabitants of Coquetdale seem to have been a right valiant and hardy fraternity, honest and fearless, well able to give good blows in defence of their possessions, for it is left on record that "the people of the said Cock-dayle be best p'pared for defence and most defensyble people of themselfes, and of the truest and best sorte of anye that do Inhabyte, endlonge, the frounter or border of the said mydle m'ches of England." The traces of these days of raid and foray are to be found in abundance all over Coquetdale, as indeed all over Northumberland, in pele-tower and barmkyn, fortified dwelling and bastle house." (**Jean F. Terry 'Northumberland, Yesterday and To-day' 1913**).

CLENNELL STREET is one of the oldest and most famous routes into Scotland. From Alwinton, this ancient road climbs northwards up onto an undulating ridge through the Cheviot Hills to reach the Border Ridge at Outer Cock Law just to the east of Windy Gyle then down to Cocklawfoot at the head of Bowmont Water in Scotland. It has been in constant use since prehistoric times, indeed the track passes numerous Bronze and Iron Age sites including hill-forts, settlements and dykes above Alwinton. In medieval times the route was referred to as the 'Magnam viam de Yarnspath' by the Cistercian monks of Newminster Abbey, near Morpeth, who held vast sheep tracks at Kidland; 'yarnspath' is thought to be derived from the Old English 'ernspeth' or eagle's path. It later became an important cross-border drovers' road that linked up with a number of other busy routes across the hills including Salter's Road and The Street, which connected Alwinton with Jedburgh via Coquetdale and Mozie Law. Used by monks, smugglers, Border Reivers, Scottish marauders and drover's throughout the centuries, Clennell Street is one of the finest green lanes in the country that offers a wonderful high-level route across open hills up to the Border Ridge; Clennell literally means 'clean hills', i.e. without trees or boundaries.

ALWINTON, pronounced 'allenton', is situated on the flat 'haugh' lands just above the confluence of the rivers Coquet and Alwin on the very edge of the Cheviot Hills; to the north and west stretch the deep valleys and rounded hills of the 'White Lands' whilst to the south and east lie the 'Black Lands' of the heather-covered sandstone Harbottle and Simonside Hills. It is the last village in Coquetdale, a remote settlement with just a handful of traditional Northumbrian cottages lining the narrow street, a fine country inn and a large green crossed by Hosedon Burn at the foot of Clennell Street; there are only a couple of isolated farms between here and the end of the narrow valley road some twelve miles away to the west at Chew Green, near the source of the Coquet. Alwinton developed at the junction of a number of important routes, most notably Clennell Street, indeed this settlement has been the 'gateway' to the Cheviots since prehistoric times. Above the village to the north are the remains of a large Iron Age fort known as Castle Hills, which enjoys superb views across the surrounding countryside. In medieval times, Alwinton grew to become the most important settlement of the 'Tens Towns of Coquetdale' during which time Castle Hills was used by the Umfravilles of Harbottle Castle, the lords of the manor, as the site of their gallows, hence its other name of Gallows Law. It later developed as an important stopping point for drovers who travelled along the ancient routes through the hills. Centuries ago, the village green would have been full of livestock and the Rose and Thistle and Red Lion Inn busy with drovers and traders. The Red Lion, a 'spirits house' that closed its doors many years ago, still overlooks the green, a finely built two-storey house that stands apart from the other single-storey traditional Northumbrian cottages. The Rose and Thistle is still going strong, an historic inn where Sir Walter Scott stayed whilst researching 'Rob Roy'; the name of the pub is said to date from the times when the Border between Scotland and England kept fluctuating so the pub would change its name to either The Rose or The Thistle, depending on which country it was in! *"A large farm-house, two excellent inns, the post office and a few cottages now constitute the ancient village of Alwinton. The "Red Lion" which was for many years kept by Hannah Jordan – a well-known hostess – has been rebuilt in modern style. The old "Rose and Thistle" on the opposite side of the road, is a favourite rendezvous for anglers, and who is there amongst the many followers of the gentle art, that yearly resort to the famous streams of Upper Coquet, but knows mine host of the "Thistle" – Mr. John Common – with his wonderful fund of stories and entertaining river-lore, for John himself is an expert with the angle."* **(David Dippie Dixon 1903)** During medieval times, the village suffered at the hands of the Reivers as well as Scottish marauders. There was once a vicar's pele tower beside the Norman church just across the river to the south at Low Alwinton, where there would have also been a sizeable settlement. As with many other upland villages, Low Alwinton has since shrunk with just a handful of cottages, some fine 19th Century limekilns, the Victorian vicarage and the Church of St Michael and All Angels remaining. This church dates back to the late 11th Century, although the site may have been used since Saxon times as a place of worship, and was enlarged in the 13th Century. It was greatly 'restored' in the 1850's with only fragments of the original Norman church surviving. It is unusual in that it is built on quite a steep slope, which requires a flight of ten steps between the nave and the chancel, beneath which is a crypt housing the tombs of the Clennell family, whilst the tombs and memorials of the Selby family can be found in the north aisle. Alwinton is famed for its annual Border Shepherds' Show held in October, the last of the seasons' traditional shows and one of the most famous shepherds' shows in Northumberland which includes traditional country sports such as wrestling, fell-running and sheepdog trials.

Alwinton

ALWINTON
to
ROTHBURY

✦

"Rising up like the crest of a massive sandstone wave, the Simonside Hills dominate the Coquet Valley and form a familiar landmark visible from almost all high ground throughout Northumberland. This undulating ridge of land is seen to best effect from the Rothbury Terraces, a series of relatively flat shelves of land that rise up in steps above the town. I followed a gravel track across the top of the Terraces, built as a carriageway for Lord Armstrong to enable him and his guests to take an afternoon 'airing'. Just off the track, a boulder strewn ridge of heather moorland offered wonderful views across the Coquet Valley towards the 'sacred mountain' with the lush Coquet Valley beneath my feet. Time for quiet reflection and contemplation. Memories flooded back of the previous five and a half days; the first glimpse of Warkworth Castle, the bracing coastal walk up to Bamburgh and the long walk through the stark yet beautiful Cheviot Hills. A walk is all about the journey not the destination and it was with great reluctance that I left the Terraces to begin the descent into Rothbury and the end of this walk."

Mark Reid
August 2003

WALK INFORMATION

Points of interest:
Victorian limekilns, Harbottle Castle and the English Middle March, ancient oak woodland, a Roman well, relics of a nunnery, flooded gravel pits and the meandering River Coquet, fortified farms, Armstrong's carriage drives and spectacular views from the Terraces across to the 'sacred mountain'.

Distance:

Alwinton to Thropton	10.5 miles
Thropton to Rothbury	3.5 miles
Total	14 miles

Time:
Allow 6 - 7 hours

Terrain:
From Alwinton to Thropton, this walk follows clear grassy / stony tracks across fields heading down through Coquetdale with some short sections of road walking along quiet country lanes. The section from Harbottle to Holystone heads through quite dense forest, although the path is clear and well-marked. From Thropton, a clear track leads up onto the Rothbury Terraces. A clear stony track sweeps to the south then east across the Terraces, into forest then quite steeply down across field paths into Rothbury.

Ascents:
Rothbury Terraces: 240 metres

Viewpoints:
The track from Low Alwinton to Harbottle.
View from Hepple Whitehead across Coquetdale.
Rothbury Terraces towards Simonside.
The descent from Addycombe into Rothbury.

FACILITIES

- -

Alwinton	Inn / B&B / P.O. / Café / Bus / Phone / Toilets / Camp
Harbottle	Inn / B&B / Bus / Phone
Holystone	P.O. / Bus / Phone
Hepple	P.O. / Bus / Phone
Thropton	Inn / B&B / Shop / P.O. / Bus / Phone / Toilets
Rothbury	Inn / B&B / Shop / P.O. / Café / Bus / Phone / Toilets / Info. / Camp

ROUTE DESCRIPTION

- -

(Map Twenty One)

Leave Alwinton along the road heading down the valley (passing the 'green' on your left) out of the village then on passing the turning for Clennell and over the bridge across the River Alwin. After this bridge, follow the road bending round to the right then take the lane to the left just after the turning (and lay-by) to St Michael and All Angels Church towards 'Low Alwinton Cottages' (BW 'Park House, Harbottle'). Follow this lane straight on over two cattle grids then climbing up passing old limekilns on to reach a gate across your path just after a group of houses (Park House). Head through the gate (metalled lane ends) and continue straight on along the grassy track ahead on to join a fence / plantation on your left that leads on to reach a gate / stile. After this gate, follow the clear grassy track gradually dropping down the hillside, through a gate into woodland. Continue along this track down through the woods then skirting around the front of a house to run alongside the River Coquet just to your right then, after about 0.25 miles where the track becomes a metalled lane, turn right over a FB beside a ford across the River Coquet. After the FB, follow the enclosed path on to join a lane opposite Harbottle Castle House, which you follow to the right to reach a T-junction in the centre of Harbottle. Turn left along the road out of the village and follow this on bending round to the left climbing up through woodland then take the stony (red colour) track to the right opposite the first cottage on your left (Rockey's Hall). Follow this track up (SP), with forest on your left and a field on your right, to reach a gate in a stone wall at the edge of the forest *(MOD Warning Signs – these relate to the MOD Ranges beyond Harbottle & Holystone Forest; the Right of Way through the Forest from here to Holystone is open at all times)*. Immediately after this gate, bear to the left along a narrow footpath (waymarker) into the bottom-corner of the forest (do not head along the track) and follow the clear narrow path diagonally through the forest out into a small clearing where you cross a stream (Seal Burn). After the stream, head on through a 'fire-break' in the forest then, after a short distance, turn right (waymarker) back into the forest. Follow the narrow path bearing to the left up through the forest, which is quite dense at first then becomes more open woodland - the path heads up to join a fence on your left along the edge of the forest. Follow this fence-line straight on, over a stile across your path and continue on along the edge of the forest then, where the open fields end on your left (with dense forest ahead of you), follow the path to the right alongside the dense forest on your left (North Wood oak woodland on your right). After a short distance, head to the left into this dense forest (waymarker) then almost immediately turn right, keeping to the edge of the dense forest, to quickly emerge from the forest at a junction of tracks (waymarker). At this junction of tracks, turn down to the left along the grassy path along the edge of the forest (silver birch trees) with open fields on your right, passing between two old stone posts then down bearing left to join a clear forest track. Turn right along this track then, after a short distance, turn left (SP 'Lady's Well'), along a track to reach a kissing gate at the end of the forest *(The path from the Forest to Lady's Well is a Forestry Commission permissive path - if this is no longer available, continue along the forest track down to join the road then follow this to the left into Holystone)*. Head straight on with the wall on your left to join a clear grassy track just to the right of the tree-shaded Lady's Well - follow this track to the right down through a gate on the edge of Holystone, after which turn left along a lane through the village, bearing left down to a T-junction at the bottom of the village. Turn left along the road ('Sharperton, Harbottle, Alwinton') and follow this on for 0.25 miles then take the FP to the right through a gate (SP 'Hepple') on across a FB across the River Coquet. After the FB, turn immediately right across the flat pastureland (River Coquet across to your right) on to quickly reach a bridle-gate in a fence.

(Map Twenty Two)

Continue straight on along a clear grassy track across flat pastures, keeping fairly close to the bottom of the bank / fence on your left, for about a mile (ignore any paths off to your left) passing the bottom of three narrow plantations coming down the bank on your left then turn left immediately before the fourth plantation (where the fence begins to curve round to the right, with the plantation running alongside this fence) over a small bridge and through a gate. After this gate, turn immediately right heading on with the forest on your right, through two bridle-gates then follow the forest bending down to the right to quickly reach another bridle-gate, after which head left gradually bearing away from the forest up across the field to a gate in a fence to the right of the rectangular plantation on the hillside. After the gate, head straight on along a grassy track across the hillside through another gate then on along a clearer track with a plantation on your left then, at this end of this plantation, turn left along a track to reach a gate after a short distance (where the plantation ends on your left). Just after this gate, turn right through another gate (waymarkers) and follow this clear track down to reach the farm buildings at West Hepple. Turn left immediately before the barns along a track then round to the right down through the farmyard then on down along the lane passing some houses on your left. Continue on then, as the lane drops downhill, take the FP to the right over a stile, bear left down across the field to a gate (SP) and onto the road on the outskirts of Hepple. Turn right along the road, over the road-bridge across the River Coquet, after which take the FP to the left (SP). Bear to the right across the field cutting off the corner to reach another stile that leads onto a road. Turn left along the road and follow this climbing uphill then swinging round to the left and levelling out near to the entrance to Hepple Whitefield. Continue straight on along the road, which soon drops down to reach the hamlet of Bickerton. Walk through the hamlet passing a small 'green' on your right, then take the track to the left immediately after Bickerton Farm (SP 'Ryehill') through a gate. Head down along the track to a kissing gate beside another gate, after which head right across the field along a grassy path to reach a stile that leads onto a track beside a large lake (Caistron Nature Reserve). Turn right along this track through a gate then continue straight on, passing several bird hides (large lake on your left), over a small bridge across Bickerton Burn after which carry straight on (still with the lake on your left and smaller lakes on your right), then follow the track as it bends sharply round to the left (passing Hide No.2) on to reach a 'crossroads' of tracks beside the 'Caistron' sign. At this crossroads, head straight on through the gate ahead (waymarker) out onto a field, then turn immediately right keeping close to the fence (and track) on your right to soon reach a bridle-gate. Head through the bridle-gate to join the clear track which you follow bending to the right then sharply round to the left (keeping to the field edge) straight on to reach a wooden gate across your path (at the end of the track) just after another flooded gravel pit on your left.

(Map Twenty Three)

After this gate, head straight on bearing slightly to the right across the open field through another gate then straight on along the track along the field-edge to join a clear track across your path. Turn right up along this track for a short distance then take the FP to the left through a gate beside a telegraph pole (SP 'Thropton'). Walk straight on with the fence on your left (Ryehill Farm up to your right) then, at the end of the field, turn left along a track through double metal gates then immediately right through another gate. Head on bearing slightly to the left across the field, keeping close to a drainage ditch on your left, to join the River Coquet, which you follow on to reach a FB across the river. Cross the FB then follow the path to the left which leaves the river behind and passes a small pond on your left then head to the right up along a grassy lane (SP) which soon becomes a metalled lane that leads up to reach the road in the centre of Thropton. Turn right along the road down through the village passing the Three Wheat Heads and over the road-bridge across Wreigh Burn then follow the main road curving up to the right towards 'Rothbury' passing the Cross Keys on your left just after which take the first turning on the left up along a lane (Physic Lane). Follow this lane up out of Thropton then where the metalled lane ends continue straight on up along the grassy track (SP 'Alnwick Road, Rothbury') up to a gate across your path. Continue straight on along the grassy track climbing gradually up - the track levels out slightly and runs alongside a plantation / stone wall on your right, which you follow bending round to the right (keeping to the grassy track). Continue along the grassy track leaving the plantation behind and follow it bending round to the left (still with the stone wall on your right) up to reach a gate across your path on the edge of the open moorland. Head through the gate then follow the clear footpath bearing to the right (ignore the track across your path) up across the moorland to join a clear gravel track (carriage drive). Turn right along this track and follow it on sweeping round to the left across the Rothbury Terraces passing a TV mast then continue on along the clear gravel track to reach a gate / bridle-gate across your path at the edge of the forest. Head straight on along the clear track climbing gently up through the forest then levelling out winding through the trees. After about 0.5 miles the track begins to drop down, gently at first then more steeply twisting sharply around a number of bends, after which the track begins to level out (fields / edge of woodland just to your right) - turn right (waymarker) along a clear bridleway almost back on yourself. Follow this clear path slanting gently down through the woods passing above a house then down to reach Hillside Road. Turn right along the road then almost immediately left along a footpath (SP). Follow the clear path bearing to the right down across fields, through kissing gates then turn left down to reach the road through a gate. Follow this road to the right (passing Armstrong's Addycombe Cottages) down into Rothbury.

MAP TWENTY ONE

MAP
TWENTY TWO

150M

219M
WREIGHILL PIKE
200M

150M

FLOODED
GRAVEL
PIT

RIVER COQUET

CAISTRON
NATURE
RESERVE

WEST HEPPLE

KIRK
HILL

HEPPLE
P.O.
B6341

TOWER

GRAVEL
WORKINGS

BICKERTON
BURN

HOLYSTONE
GRANGE

WOODHOUSES
BASTLE

BICKERTON

150M

FORT
HAREHAUGH,
HILL
150M

150M

200M

SWINDON
HILL

WITCHY
NEUK
FORT

HEPPLE
WHITEFIELD

GRASSLEES
BURN

SIMONSIDE HILLS

400M

150M

200M

440M
TOSSON HILL

400M

MAP
TWENTY THREE

HARBOTTLE is an ancient village with a fascinating history that belies its sleepy appearance for this was once the home of a powerful family that held sway in this troubled Border country for four centuries, ruling it almost as an independent region. *"Apart from the commanding site on which it stands, amid the wilds of Upper Coquetdale, there cluster around the old grey ruins of Harbottle Castle many thrilling associations, full of interest to all who take pleasure in the history of this northern county."* **(David Dippie Dixon 'Upper Coquetdale' 1903).** The name of the village is said to be derived from the Old English 'here-botl' that roughly translates as the 'abode of the army', which may indicate that there was a pre-Conquest defensive structure here protected by the wide loop of the River Coquet. In the early 12th Century, Robert de Umfraville, one of William the Conqueror's loyal knights, was given the Liberty of Redesdale, a huge swathe of land along the disputed Border that included Redesdale as well as much of Upper Coquetdale and soon set about building a timber motte and bailey castle at Elsdon to protect these lands. The Liberty of Redesdale was an extremely important area as it acted as a 'buffer' between England and Scotland with several busy roads passing through en route to Scotland. They soon abandoned their castle at Elsdon in favour of the more strategic site at Harbottle on the orders of Henry II who was keen to strengthen the Border defences after he had regained his northern counties from the Scots, although some say the Umfravilles moved northwards because Redesdale was too lawless! Building work began on Harbottle Castle in around 1157 under the watchful eye of Odinel de Umfraville, Lord of Redesdale. The castle was designed to guard the important routes through Coquetdale over to Scotland, in particular Clennell Street, however, it was taken by the Scots in 1174 when William I of Scotland invaded Northumberland then again, despite the strengthening of the keep in the 13th Century, by Robert Bruce following his famous victory over the English at Bannockburn in 1314. During this turbulent period, the Umfravilles exercised almost regal powers in this area with their own courts, gaol and gallows. *"Many a dismal sight must the dark dungeons of Harbottle have witnessed in these cruel times, for within them were confined prisoners – and they would be very numerous – who were taken in the Liberty of Redesdale.*

The castle had been so much ruined by the Scottish wars, that in 1336 Gilbert de Umfraville obtained permission to transfer them to his castle at Prudhoe." **(William Weaver Tomlinson 'Comprehensive Guide to Northumberland' 1888).** The castle grew to become one of the most important Border fortresses during medieval times, however, the Umfravilles lost their Liberty of Redesdale in 1436 and the area, which previously formed part of the English East March, became the English Middle March with Harbottle as its administrative centre, supported by the 'Ten Towns of Coquetdale'. The 'Marches' were established by Edward I to bring order to this region after his decision in 1292 to impose John Balliol as 'king' of Scotland thus effectively claiming the throne for himself as 'overlord', which resulted in three centuries of bloodshed between the two countries. The northern English counties were divided into the East March (Northumberland), later split to form the Middle March, and the West March (Cumberland), with Wardens appointed by the King to impose law and order thus making this region a virtual military zone, although this did very little to prevent Scottish attacks nor did it discourage the Border Reivers who took advantage of the lawlessness. In fact, during the early 16th Century the Warden of the Middle March, Thomas Dacre, actually made things worse due to his remit of army commander, police chief and political agitator rolled into one; many of his schemes which were meant to help govern this area actually inflamed the situation leading to decades of bloody lawlessness and reiving. The Reivers were family clans, known as 'Riding Surnames', who terrorised neighbouring valleys stealing livestock and possessions; some notable names included Armstrong, Hall, Forster, Elliot, Robson, Noble and Carleton. For 300 years they made this region almost uninhabitable, with local people left to defend themselves, hence the large number of pele towers and bastle houses that were built in virtually every Northumbrian town and village; the Border Reivers also left their mark in our language with words such as 'bereave' and 'blackmail'. The castle's most famous moment came in 1515 when the pregnant Margaret Tudor, sister of Henry VIII and widow of James IV of Scotland who had been killed in the Battle of Flodden two years earlier, was granted asylum at the castle along with her second husband the Earl of Angus. She gave birth to a daughter, also called Margaret, who became the mother-in-law of Mary Queen of Scots and grandmother of James VI of Scotland who was crowned James I of England in 1603, thus uniting the two crowns and bringing to an end centuries of bloodshed. The castle was strengthened in the mid 16th Century with, it is said, stones taken from Holystone Priory, however, by the end of the century it was in ruins. After the Union of the Crowns in 1603, castles were no longer required so it was sold by the Crown to the Widdrington family who subsequently built the 'new' Harbottle Castle at the east end of the village using stones from the medieval castle. This fine house was rebuilt in 1829 by the famous architect John Dobson for Thomas Clennell, who then owned the estate - in the centre of Harbottle is an ornate Victorian Gothic drinking fountain, known as the Clennell Memorial Fountain, which boasts a wonderful inscription: *"She devoted the powers of an active mind, the impulses of a generous heart, and the industry of a busy life to the welfare and happiness of the inhabitants of Harbottle and the neighbourhood. To perpetuate her name and virtues they erected this fountain August 1880."* The village of Harbottle developed in the protective shadow of the castle and consists of a delightful long single street of attractive 18th and 19th century houses and cottages, a traditional Northumbrian country inn, a former National School built in 1834 as well as an old Presbyterian Chapel. Harbottle was once renowned for its healthy inhabitants and boasted one of the lowest death rates in the country! During the late 19th Century the local doctor, Dr Richardson, wrote a letter to The Times highlighting the very low mortality rate and long life expectancy of people in the parish *"...The inhabitants have abundance of plain substantial food, excellent water, good residences as a rule, and regular but not severe work in a pure bracing atmosphere, and are highly intelligent, and generally abstemious."* Above the village to the south and east rise the craggy Harbottle Hills, which are crowned by the famous Drake Stone, a huge outcrop of sandstone some 30-ft high. This rock is thought to have been used in ancient times by the Druids during their rituals, indeed, up until the early 1800's local superstition was still so strong that sick children were passed over it to be cured. Just beyond the Drake Stone is Harbottle Lake, a small expanse of water hidden away on the wide ridge of heather moorland. Many years ago, workmen came up here to drain the lake but fled in terror when they heard a voice seemingly emanating from the water…

Let alone, let alone,
Or I'll drown Harbottle
And the Peels and the bonny Holystone.

Harbottle Castle

OTTERBURN TRAINING AREA covers a vast area to the west and south of Harbottle, some 58,000 acres of wilderness including large tracts of desolate moorland and uninhabited valleys that are used to train over 30,000 soldiers each year. The area to the north of the River Coquet (upstream of Alwinton) is used for 'dry training' where soldiers use blanks and pyrotechnics; the paths are always open within this area, however, you may encounter troops in full combat gear out on manoeuvres, which certainly adds a different dimension to your walk. The area to the south of the Coquet, from its source down to Holystone then south towards Elsdon, is used as a live firing range. For reasons of safety, this area is subject to Byelaws and public access is restricted; when the red flags are flying the whole area is closed. The message is: observe notices, do not stray from the path and never pick up any objects lying on the ground. It is quite amazing to think that this training area covers a fifth of the National Park, a fact that sometimes attracts criticism from conservation groups, however, the Army were here first! In 1911, the War Office bought 19,000 acres of land in Redesdale as an artillery range, which was extended during the Second World War to create the largest live firing range in the country. In fact, soldiers have been here for almost 2,000 years as two Roman roads crossed this area including the important military road of Dere Street, as well as numerous forts and camps. Ironically, the fact that much of this training area has been closed off from the public for so long, coupled with low intensity farming methods, means that it stands as some of the last wilderness in the country and an important habitat for wildlife. Our route follows Public Footpaths from Rockey's Hall near Harbottle through Harbottle Wood and North Wood to Holystone; this path is open at all times - the red flags and warning signs relate to the area beyond the forest (flags are sited for visibility rather than marking the edge of the danger area). Harbottle Wood forms part of the vast Holystone Forest, owned and managed by the Forestry Commission. Parts of the forest are quite dense with large tracts of spruce and lodgepole pine, however, through careful felling and planting the forest is well managed with a good mix of trees that has helped maintain a number of important habitats; the forest is also managed for recreation with waymarked paths and picnic sites. North Wood is a rare example of an ancient coppiced oak forest, where stumps were allowed to grow after the tree had been felled, which were then used to make charcoal for iron smelting. The trees were last coppiced some 60 years ago and the woodland is now protected as a Nature Reserve.

LADY'S WELL lies hidden amongst a small copse of trees, a truly spiritual oasis of peace that has been used since the earliest times as a place of worship. A large yet shallow rectangular basin of crystal clear spring water - 560 gallons are said to bubble up every minute - was walled round to create the present cistern in medieval or perhaps even

Roman times for this spring was used as a watering place beside the Roman road between Bremenium in Redesdale and the Devil's Causeway. After the Romans left these shores, it was used as an early Christian baptism site, indeed, it is sometimes referred to St Ninian's Well after the 5th Century 'Apostle of the Border' who possibly visited and consecrated this old Roman pagan site. St Ninian was Scotland's earliest known saint who founded the first monastery in Scotland at Whithorn in the late 4th Century. Although shrouded in mystery, he spent his life converting pagans throughout Scotland and Northumbria and is associated with several wells beside Roman roads. The most famous story associated with Lady's Well is that of St Paulinus, who came to Northumbria in the early 7th Century as a guest of Edwin, King of Northumbria to preach Christianity in his kingdom. It is said that during Easter 627AD St Paulinus baptised 3,000 Northumbrian pagans here, although this is disputed as some historians claim that he was in York that day! The name of Lady's Well came into use during the late 12th Century when an Augustinian Priory of nuns dedicated to St Mary the Virgin was established in the neighbouring village of Holystone. Lady's Well was repaired in the 18th and 19th Centuries and is adorned with a simple Celtic cross as well as a statue of St Paulinus. The statue is said to stand on the original altar stone, or Holy Stone, used by Christians over a millennium ago. For almost 2,000 years the well provided drinking water for the village, until it was closed due to 'regulations' in 1998!

HOLYSTONE is an attractive, sleepy village set on the edge of the vast Holystone Forest. Old houses crowd round a small road junction in the centre of the village where a bold red sign points rather ominously towards the 'Ranges', while the occasional rumble of distant explosions and gunfire give the village a rather strange atmosphere! Tucked away just off this junction is the former Salmon Inn, one of Coqetdale's most famous pubs that sadly called last orders for the last time recently. A century ago, Holystone was quite a sizeable village with a corn mill (the mill race can still be seen running through the village), farms, blacksmiths' shop, various crafts and tradesmen, school, church as well as the pub. *"At present the aspect of the village is decidedly antique, and* *characteristic of the district. A number of irregularly-built cottages, many of them thatched and falling into ruins, and, to all appearance, constructed out of the materials of some ancient tower, the space enclosed by them partly transformed into little gardens; a small church and graveyard, an old water-mill, a farmstead, and inn; the whole clustering together on the north bank of a crystal stream, at the base of craggy hills, which rise on the west and south to a height of 800 feet."* **(W. W. Tomlinson 1888).** In medieval times, it was home to a small Augustinian Priory of nuns, one of the earliest in the country established here in around 1124 by Robert de Umfraville near the holy site of St Ninian's Well. Despite being granted lands throughout the area, the Priory was often impoverished due to constant attacks by the Scots, particularly during the 14th Century. The Priory was dissolved in 1536 as part of the Dissolution of the Monasteries. Fragments remain of the medieval church within the present Church of St Mary the Virgin, the nave of which was built in the 1840's upon the foundations of the chancel of the much larger Priory Church. There is another holy well at Holystone dedicated to St Mungo, which can be found alongside the lane just to the south of the village housed in a simple 19th Century water fountain. St Mungo followed 'in the footsteps' of St Ninian as he preached Christianity initially throughout Scotland then further a-field during the 6th Century. Properly called St Kentigern ('Mungo' was his nickname and means 'dear friend'), he founded a church above the River Clyde and in doing so founded the city of Glasgow. He also spent many years in Wales where, it is said, he met St David and founded a religious centre that grew to become the cathedral city of St Asaph; his disciple Asaph was left in charge when St Mungo returned to Scotland. *"It is of some interest to trace the route of the Glasgow saint, Kentigern, on his way to St. Asaph, by the names attached to wells throughout the county. Somewhere near Wooler there is a "Mungo's Well;" we have "St. Mungo's Well" at Holystone; and at Simonburn, on North Tyne, there is also "St. Mungo's Well. The beautiful well at Holystone, known to us as "The Lady's Well," also described as "The Well of St Paulinus," was formerly "St Ninian's Well." There appears, therefore, to have been from very early times a religious halo around Holystone; and no doubt the pious Umfraville of seven centuries ago, attracted by the situation and the sanctity of the spot, the abundant supply of pure water, and its close proximity to the* *river Coquet, made choice of this romantic spot amid the hills of Upper Coquet for the founding of the convent."* **(David Dippie Dixon 1903).**

Lady's Well

HEPPLE is situated on a spur of land above the meandering River Coquet, with old stone houses lining the main road over to Redesdale via the valley of Grasslees Burn. This side-valley provides one of the few relatively low-level routes across the hills between Coquetdale and Redesdale and was a favourite route for Reivers. There are numerous bastle houses in this area such as the superb Vicar's Pele at Elsdon as well as simpler examples at The Raw, High Shaw, the Ironhouse, Craig and Woodhouses. Woodhouses Bastle is one of the finest surviving examples in Northumberland, and can be clearly seen across the valley from the footpath that leads up across Kirk Hill towards West Hepple Farm, sheltered by belts of trees on a sloping hillside beside the distinguished house of Holystone Grange. As the name suggest, a Norman chapel once stood on Kirk Hill surrounded by a small settlement, however, this church was destroyed by Scottish raiders during the Border Troubles, although the exact date is unknown. The ruins were cleared away in the 18th Century and a cross erected on the site, with the stone being recycled to build the adjacent farmhouse of West Hepple. The cross has since disappeared, although the original Norman font can be found in the 'new' Christ Church along the main road, a plain and simple late 19th Century church, which boasts a brightly painted interior. When the ruins of the old Hepple Chapel were cleared, a 13th Century tombstone was discovered with a long and unusual inscription on it that possibly belonged to Lady Tailbois, wife of the Lord of Hepple; part of the inscription read:

I loved my Lord, obeyed my king,
And kept my conscience clear,
Which Death disarmeth of his sting,
And Christians all endear.

In medieval times, Hepple was the centre of a small but important barony held directly from the king by the Lord of the Manor that included, along with Hepple, the villages of Bickerton, Great Tosson, Little Tosson and Sharperton. As with the neighbouring Liberty of Redesdale, the Barony of Hepple had the rights of capital punishment as well as other privileges, designed to deter Scottish raiders and the notorious Reivers. During the 13th and 14th Centuries the barony was held by the Tailbois family, who were succeeded by the Ogle family. In the mid 14th Century, the lords of Hepple built themselves a large pele tower in the village, which formed part of a string of pele towers down through Coquetdale. At one time, the tower was occupied by Sir Robert Ogle, Warden of the East Marches, on behalf of the Earl of Northumberland; the Ogles were a powerful Northumbrian family who held lands throughout Coquetdale including a pele tower at Great Tosson. This family is said to be one of the oldest in the county dating back to pre-Conquest times who were, by all accounts, also renowned Reivers! At one time, Hepple Tower could call upon a small garrison of twenty men at arms who were ready to defend the barony. In more recent times, when workmen were looking for a ready supply of dressed stone to build the neighbouring farmhouse in the late 18th Century, they tried in vain to loot stones but were prevented by the skills of the medieval masons who had built a very stout tower! The ruins of Hepple Tower can still be seen just off the road at the east end of the village (private grounds). From Hepple, our route follows a quiet country lane climbing up across the flanks of Swindon Hill, from where there are superb views back across the wide valley with the Coquet meandering across flat pastureland. *"In the flat green bend of the river below the dalesmen of Rede and Coquet used to gather for cock-fighting and racing, pursuits which usually ended in cudgel play."* **(A. Mee 'The King's England: Northumberland' 1952).** The quiet country lane skirts Swindon Hill then leads down to the hamlet of Bickerton, which once formed part of the Barony of Hepple. This attractive hamlet has a small green as well as interesting farm buildings including an old horse-gin, which utilised horse power to drive farm machinery; 'horse gin' is a corruption of 'horse engine'.

CAISTRON NATURE RESERVE forms an attractive feature along the floor of the valley, a shining example of how quarrying can actually enhance the landscape. For over fifty years, the extraction of sand and gravel along this stretch of the River Coquet has left several large flooded gravel pits, which have been transformed to create an award-winning private nature reserve. Through careful landscaping, a variety of habitats have been created including shallow wetland areas to attract wading birds, an irregular shoreline that provides ideal nesting sites a well as belts of trees and vegetation to encourage wildlife. Caistron has matured into a haven for wildlife and birds with over 190 recorded species of birds, including an amazing 70 species in one day! This is still a working quarry with gravel pits at its western end; as extraction gradually moves upstream, the redundant workings are then restored to form part of the Nature Reserve.

THROPTON lies sheltered beneath the sandstone hills of the Rothbury Terraces near the confluence of Wreigh Burn and the Coquet, facing across the broad valley towards the Simonside Hills. To the north sweeps the undulating hills and pastures of the Vale of Whittingham (pronounced 'whitting-jam'), which forms a broad swathe of fertile farmland around the foothills of the Cheviots. These are the Cementstone Group of rocks, which form a distinctive divide between the central sandstone Black Lands and the White Lands of the Cheviot Hills. These rocks consist of layer upon layer of sandstone, clay, shale and limestone deposited over 300 million years ago by torrents of water flowing down from the newly created volcanic landmass of what are now the Cheviot Hills into a surrounding deep sea. Millions of years later, a thick band of sandstone was deposited above these Cementstone rocks in a huge river delta, which was subsequently pushed and tilted by a series of massive earth movements that created the central sandstone hills with their west-facing escarpments. The Cementstone rocks are easily weathered and so have produced the fertile undulating lands around the eastern edge of the well-defined Cheviot range. *"The villagers take great delight in their gardens, while the richness of the soil helps to produce flowers, fruits and vegetables of superb quality, as may be seen at the village Autumn Show, held annually, in the month of October. Thropton is said to have been the first place in this part of Coquetdale where potatoes were grown. The village is so famous for the excellent quality of that most useful vegetable that it is sometimes jocularly called "tatie toon," and an old villager once remarked that "It wis ne use onybody gan to leeve at Thropton if they cuddent taak aboot taties."* **(David Dippie Dixon 1903).** People have been living in this area since prehistoric times as there are two well preserved Iron Age hill-forts just above the village to the east. Thropton was probably first settled by Anglo-Saxon farmers as the suffix 'ton' indicates, however, the village was first mentioned in the 13th Century when it formed part of the Lordship of Rothbury. The linear layout of the village has changed little since medieval times with houses lining the wide street, as well as a cluster of houses around the junction with the Whittingham road above the hog-backed bridge across Wreigh Burn, which was built in 1810. Just above this bridge is All Saint Catholic Church, which dates from the early 19th Century although it stands on the site of an older chapel that was originally attached to Thropton Old Hall. This Old Hall, which may have also incorporated a bastle house, was sadly demolished in 1811 to make way for the present Presbytery, a well-proportioned house set back behind a high stone wall. Thropton has always been a centre for Catholicism, indeed, the Old Faith never really died out in this area even during the dark days of the Reformation. Thropton actually boasts two more dedicated places of worship including the United Reformed Church, originally a Presbyterian church that dates from 1863, easily identifiable by its unusual Gothic porchway topped by an ornate turret, whilst along the Cartington road is a small timber-built Church of England chapel of the early 1900's. Further up through the village beyond the 18th Century Three Wheat Heads Inn is The Peels, a fine example of a large bastle house that is still used as a house. Thropton Bastle dates back to the 15th Century and once could call upon sixteen armed men to dispel any Scottish attack. Just across Wreigh Burn on the edge of the village set amongst wooded gardens is Wreighburn House, a large predominantly 18th Century house that stands on the site of a medieval hospital. Founded in the 13th Century, this hospital is believed to have been under the control of the Knights Hospitallers until it closed following the Dissolution of the Monasteries; all that remains is a stone with a cross carved onto it that may be a medieval grave slab.

Thropton

ROTHBURY TERRACES rise up above the town, a continuation of the central sandstone hills that sweep through the heart of Northumberland. Beneath these wide natural shelves of heath-clad moorland, the River Coquet has carved a deep, steep-sided gorge through the hills. Considering their modest height, the Rothbury Terraces offer superb views of Coquetdale, especially from the well-made gravel tracks that sweep around the hillsides. During the late 19th Century this whole area formed part of the vast Cragside Estate, owned by Lord Armstrong, who had these tracks laid out as carriage drives so that his Lordship and his guests could enjoy an afternoon 'airing' across the heather moorland hill-tops - nothing too strenuous, mind! Cragside House is now in the care of The National Trust, but the Rothbury Terraces are still owned by the Armstrong family of Bamburgh Castle. Below the gravel carriage drive, just before the TV transmitter, on a flat shelf of land are the remains of a large Iron Age hill-fort known as Old Rothbury. Traces of stone hut circles can be seen within a large defensive double ditch, whilst all around are numerous other prehistoric remains including cup and ring marked stones and Bronze Age clearance cairns.

The descent from the Terraces is superb with Simonside rising above the rooftops and Coquetdale spread out beneath your feet. The joy and sense of achievement at seeing Rothbury after six days is tinged with sadness for this marks the end of the walk and the end of your journey through Northumberland... but this is a journey that can be re-lived time and again through the countless memories you will now take with you forever.

BIBLIOGRAPHY

The following books are listed as follows: author, title, date first published and publisher.

Walter White, 'Northumberland and The Border', 1859, Chapman and Hall.

William Weaver Tomlinson, 'Comprehensive Guide to Northumberland', 1888, William H. Robinson.

David Dippie Dixon, 'Upper Coquetdale', 1903, Robert Redpath.

A. G. Bradley, 'The Romance of Northumberland', 1908, Methuen.

J. S. Fletcher, 'The Enchanting North', 1908, Eveleigh Nash.

Jean F. Terry, 'Northumberland, Yesterday and To-day', 1913, Andrew Reid & Co Ltd.

Iris Wedgwood, 'Northumberland and Durham', 1932, Faber & Faber Ltd.

Rt Hon W. Ormsby Gore MP, 'Ancient Monuments, Volume 1 Northern England', 1936, HMSO.

Douglas Goldring, 'A Tour in Northumbria', 1938, George Allen & Unwin Ltd.

Herbert Honeyman, 'Northumberland', 1949, Robert Hale Ltd.

A. Mee, 'The King's England: Northumberland', 1952, Hodder & Stoughton.

Nikolaus Pevsner, 'The Buildings of England: Northumberland', 1959, Penguin. *Extracts reproduced with permission from Yale University Press.*

Nancy Ridley, 'Portrait of Northumberland', 1965, Robert Hale Ltd.

Nancy Ridley, 'Northumbrian Heritage', 1968, Robert Hale Ltd.

J. Philipson, 'Northumberland National Park', 1969, HMSO.

Bruce Allsopp & Ursula Clark, 'Historic Architecture of Northumberland', 1969, Oriel Press.

John Hadfield (Editor), 'The Shell Guide to England', 1970, Michael Joseph.

Nigel Tranter, 'The Illustrated Portrait of the Border Country', 1972, Robert Hale Ltd.

Robert Newton, 'The Northumberland Landscape', 1972, Hodder & Stoughton.

Frank Atkinson, 'Life and Tradition in Northumberland and Durham', 1977, J. M. Dent & Sons Ltd.

Frank Graham, 'The Old Halls, Houses and Inns of Northumberland', 1977, F. Graham.

Joan Williams, 'Walks in Coquetdale', 1986, Northumberland National Park.

Various, 'AA / Ordnance Survey Leisure Guide: Northumbria', 1987, Ordnance Survey.

Ian Smith, 'Northumbrian Coastline', 1988, Sandhill Press.

Lynn Pearson, 'The Northumbrian Pub', 1989, Sandhill Press.

D. Crystal (Editor), 'The Cambridge Encyclopaedia', 1990, Cambridge University Press.

Frank Duerden, 'Best Walks in Northumberland', 1990, Constable.

Various authors, 'Cragside', 1992, The National Trust.

A. B. E. Clark, 'Brinkburn Priory', 1992, English Heritage.

James Gracie (Editor), 'Hidden Places of Northumberland and Durham', 1992, Travel Publishing.

Henry Summerson, 'Dunstanburgh Castle', 1993, English Heritage.

Stephen Rickerby, 'Best Pub Walks in Northumbria', 1994, Sigma Leisure.

Henry Summerson, 'Warkworth Castle', 1995, English Heritage.

David Winpenny, 'AA / Ordnance Survey: Northumbria and Hadrian's Wall', 1996, Ordnance Survey.

Tony Hopkins, 'Land of the far Horizons', 1997, Northumberland National Park Authority.

Edward Baker, 'Walks in the Secret Kingdom', 1998, Sigma Leisure.

Lee Frost, 'Northumbria', 1998, Constable.

Roly Smith, 'Insight Compact Guides: Northumbria', 1998, Apa Publications.

Alan Hall, 'Walking in Northumberland', 1998, Cicerone Press.

Rob Talbot & Robin Whiteman, 'Northumbria', 1998, Weidenfeld & Nicolson.

M. Scott Weightman, 'The Coast of Northumberland', 1998, Pitkin Guides.

Lydia Speakman, 'Northumberland Towns & Villages', 2000, Sigma Leisure.

Brian Conduit & John Brooks, 'Northumberland, the Borders and Hadrian's Wall, Pathfinder Guide', 2000, Jarrold.

Mr F. Watson Armstrong, 'Bamburgh Castle', 2001, Jarrold.

Mark Reid, 'Town Trails, Northumbria', 2002, InnWay Publications.

Grace Hickling, 'Farne Islands', 2002, The National Trust.

Tony Hopkins, 'Northumberland, The Official National Park Guide', 2002, Pevensey Guides.

Roger Protz (Editor), 'Good Beer Guide', 2004, CAMRA

Alisdair Aird (Editor), 'The Good Pub Guide', 2004, Ebury Press.

LOG BOOK

· ·

"Drinking in the scenery"

Visit as many of the forty-eight pubs along The Inn Way…to Northumberland as possible and keep a record of your progress with this Log Book.

Send your completed Log Book to the address below to receive your free 'Inn Way Certificate' (please include a SAE as well as your name and address, we will return this Log Book with your certificate). Photocopies of this Log Book will not be accepted.

Inn Way Merchandise

If you would like to purchase an 'Inn Way Certificate' then please write to us for a copy of 'The Inn Way' colour brochure:

'The Inn Way' books, 'Drinking in the scenery' outdoor fleeces, polo shirts & T-shirts, 'Inn Way' fabric badges, 'Inn Way' Certificates, 'Inn Way' postcards featuring the pen and ink drawings from the books plus much more…

InnWay Publications
102 LEEDS ROAD
HARROGATE
HG2 8HB

www.innway.co.uk

LOG BOOK

. . . .

Day One   **Time of visit**   **Date**   **Remarks**

1. Newcastle Hotel, Rothbury

2. Turks Head, Rothbury

3. Queens Head, Rothbury

4. Railway Hotel, Rothbury

6. Coquet Vale Hotel, Rothbury

7. Anglers Arms, Weldon Bridge

8. Northumberland Arms, West Thirston

9. Stags Head, Felton

10. Warkworth House Hotel, Warkworth

11. Black Bull, Warkworth

12. Masons Arms, Warkworth

13. Hermitage Inn, Warkworth

14. Sun Hotel, Warkworth

Day Two

15. Hope and Anchor, Alnmouth

16. Sun Inn, Alnmouth

17. Saddle Hotel, Alnmouth

18. Red Lion Inn, Alnmouth

19. Schooner Hotel, Alnmouth

20. Fishing Boat Inn, Boulmer

21. Jolly Fisherman, Craster

22. Sportsman Hotel, Embleton

23. Dunstanburgh Castle Hotel, Embleton

24. Greys Inn, Embleton

25. Blue Bell Inn, Embleton

Day Three

26. Ship Inn, Low Newton-by-the-Sea

27. Craster Arms, Beadnell

28. New Beadnell Towers Hotel, Beadnell

29. Olde Ship Hotel, Seahouses

30. Black Swan Inn, Seahouses

31. Schooner Inn, Seahouses

32. Harbour Inn, Seahouses

33. Victoria Hotel, Bamburgh

34. Mizen Head Hotel, Bamburgh

35. Lord Crewe Arms, Bamburgh

36. Castle Hotel, Bamburgh

Day Four

37. Apple Inn, Lucker

38. White Swan Inn, Warenford

39. Percy Arms Hotel, Chatton

40. Tankerville Arms, Wooler

41. Red Lion, Wooler

42. Black Bull Hotel, Wooler

43. Angel Inn, Wooler

44. Wheatsheaf Hotel, Wooler

45. Anchor Inn, Wooler

Day Five

46. Rose and Thistle, Alwinton

Day Six

47. Star Inn, Harbottle

48. Three Wheat Heads, Thropton

49. Cross Keys, Thropton:

Name ....

Address ....

....

Date completed ....

Don't forget the A4 SAE

Northumberland National Park

Sustainable Tourism

A percentage of the profit from the sale of this book will be donated to local conservation projects within the National Park; money raised will fund activities such as habitat creation, wildlife surveys or tree planting.

Northumberland National Park is one of the most important landscapes in the country in terms of tranquillity, wildlife and archaeology. The National Park Authority works with local people to conserve and enhance the landscape and provide facilities and information for visitors.

By enjoying this walk, appreciating the scenery and supporting local businesses you have already made a positive contribution to the upkeep of the National Park.

Thank you for visiting Northumberland - we look forward to seeing you again sometime.

www.northumberland-national-park.org.uk